NUT**SHELLS**

Employment Law

D1428540

YOU'VE GOT IT
CRACKED

Nutcases – your essential revision and starter guides

- Provides you with in-depth case analysis of the facts, principles and decision of the most important cases in an area of law

- Incorporates colour to help distinguish cases and legislation and aid ease of use

- Presents the text in bite-size chunks and includes bullets where appropriate to aid navigation, assimilation and retention of information

- Breaks the subject down into key topics to enable you to easily identify and concentrate on particular topics

- Opens each chapter with a short introduction to outline the key concepts covered and condense complex and important information

- Highlights Court of Appeal and House of Lords cases to enable you to easily identify the relative significance of the cases examined

- Includes boxed "think points" at the end of each chapter providing further case analysis

- Fully indexed by individual cases and topics

Available from all good booksellers

NUT**SHELLS**

Employment Law

FIFTH EDITION

by
ANDREW C. BELL
Visiting Lecturer in Law, Nottingham Law School

SWEET & MAXWELL

 THOMSON REUTERS

First edition – 2001
Second edition – 2003
Third edition – 2006
Fourth edition – 2009

Published in 2012 by Sweet & Maxwell
part of Thomson Reuters (Professional) UK Limited
(Registered in England and Wales, Company No. 1679046.
Registered Office and address for service:
Aldgate House, 33 Aldgate High Street, London EC3N 1DL)

For further information on our products and services, visit
www.sweetandmaxwell.co.uk

Typeset by YHT Ltd
Printed in the Netherlands by
Ten Brink, Meppel

No natural forests were destroyed to make this product;
only farmed timber was used and re-planted

A CIP catalogue record for this book is available from the British Library.

ISBN: 9780414022973
Thomson Reuters and the Thomson Reuters logo are trademarks of Thomson Reuters.
Sweet & Maxwell® is a registered trademark of Thomson Reuters (Professional) UK Limited.

Contents

v

Using this Book

Welcome to our new look NUTSHELLS revision series. We have revamped and improved the existing design and layout and added new features, according to student feedback.

NEW DETAILED TABLE OF CONTENTS for easy navigation.

REDESIGNED TABLES OF CASES AND LEGISLATION for easy reference.

NEW CHAPTER INTRODUCTIONS to outline
the key concepts covered and condense
complex and important information.

Other Statutory R.

NATIONAL MINIMUM WAGE AC1

The National Minimum Wage Act 19
minimum hourly rate of pay for all v
tate to determine and amer
are set: on-

**DEFINITION CHECKPOINTS,
EXPLANATION OF KEY CASES AND
LEGISLATION HIGHLIGHTERS**
to highlight important information.

.iate between employee.
ed "independent contractors", wi
aws and rules.

LEGISLATION HIGHLIGHTER

EMPLOYMENT RIGHTS ACT 1996 SECTION :

DEFINITIONS AND TESTS

Statutory definition
)ften it is not difficult to identify an e'
ts Act 1996 (ERA) states, "In this
red into or works under

are the other provision-
contract of employment.

KEY CASE

CARMICHAEL V NATIONAL POWER PLC [1(
Mrs Carmichael worked as a guide for I
required" basis, showing groups of vi'
tion. She worked some hours most we
wore a company uniform, was some
vehicle, and enjoyed many of the b
question for the court to determin
"umbrella" or "global" emplo\
h she worked and th

PUBLIC INTEREST DISCL

The purpose of the Act is to prote,
employers in cases where the worker
of his employer.

The Act protects a worker again
or any other detriment, if the reason c
the worker has made a "protected d'

The term "worker" is given an ext
(a) Those working under a c'
1996).
Those working '

DIAGRAMS, FLOWCHARTS AND OTHER DIAGRAMMATIC REPRESENTATION to clarify and condense complex and important information and breakup the text.

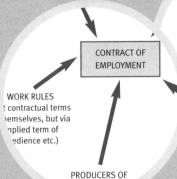

Figure 1 Court and Tribunal System

House of Lords ━ ━ ━ ━

COURT OF APPEAL
(CIVIL DIVISION)

↑

EMPLOYMENT APPEAL
TRIBUNAL

CONTRACT OF
EMPLOYMENT

WORK RULES
t contractual terms
emselves, but via
nplied term of
edience etc.)

PRODUCERS OF
COLLECTIVE

END OF CHAPTER REVISION CHECKLISTS outlining what you should now know and understand.

Chapter Checklist

You should now know and unders

- the three heads of claim for
- issues regarding the choice of
- the role of the independent e:
- what is meant by "pay".

QUESTION AND AN

END OF CHAPTER QUESTION AND ANSWER SECTION with advice on relating knowledge to examination performance, how to approach the question, how to structure the answer, the pitfalls (and how to avoid them!) and how to get the best marks.

QUESTION AND ANSWER

The Question

David and Emily are employed as machi worked for them for one and a half yea

Emily discovers that David earns £9.0 paid £8.50 per hour. She also disc employed by a subsidiary of XCo ir

HANDY HINTS AND USEFUL WEBSITES
– revision and examination tips and
advice relating to the subject features
at the end of the book, along with a list
of Useful Websites.

HANDY HINTS

Examination questions in employmei
either essay questions or problem ques
format and in what is required of the ex
of question in turn.

Students usually prefer one type
normally opting for the problem ques
examinations are usually set in a wa'
least one of each style of question

Very few, if any, questions
ows about a topic, and it i
make a p

USEFUL WEBSITES

British and Irish Legal Information Ir
www.bailii.org

Court of Justice of the European Comr
http://curia.europa.eu/en/index.htm

Daily Law Notes
www.lawreports.co.uk/indexdln.ht

Employment Appeals Tribur
nlovmentanc

NEW COLOUR CODING throughout to
help distinguish cases and legislation
from the narrative. At the first mention,
cases are highlighted in colour and
italicised and legislation is highlighted
in colour and emboldened.

w has d
are an ethnic group (*Seia*
ypsies are an ethnic group (*CRE*
Rastafarians are not an ethnic group
ment [1993] I.R.L.R. 284)
(d) Jehovah's Witnesses are not an ethnic o
Norwich City College case 1502237/97)
(e) RRA covers the Welsh (*Gwynedd CC v Jone*
(f) Both the Scots and the English are covere
"national origins" but not by "ethnic or
Board v Power [1997], *Boyce v British Ai*

It should be noted that Sikhs, Jews, Je
ians are also protected on '
Equality (Religion or P

Table of Cases

Table of Statutes

Table of Abbreviations

ACAS	Advisory, Conciliation and Arbitration Service
CCT	Compulsory Competitive Tendering
CRE	Commission for Racial Equality
DDA	Disability Discrimination Act 1995
EA	Employment Act 2002
EAT	Employment Appeals Tribunal
ECHR	European Court of Human Rights
ECJ	European Court of Justice
EDT	Effective Date of Termination
EOC	Equal Opportunities Commission
ERA	Employment Rights Act 1996
ERelA	Employment Relations Act 1999
EqPA	Equal Pay Act 1970
ETO	Economic Technical or Organisational (reason)
GOQ	Genuine Occupational Qualification
HRA	Human Rights Act 1998
HSE	Health and Safety Executive
HSWA	Health and Safety at Work Act 1974
NMWA	National Minimum Wage Act 1998
PIDA	Public Interest Disclosure Act 1998
RRA	Race Relations Act 1976
SDA	Sex Discrimination Act 1975
SI	Statutory Instrument
SOSR	Some Other Substantial Reason
TULR(C)A	Trade Union and Labour Relations (Consolidation) Act 1992
TUPE	Transfer of Undertakings (Protection of Employment) Regulations 1981

Introduction

SOURCES OF EMPLOYMENT LAW

All of your authorities to support any proposition in employment law will be either statute or case law, and often a combination of both. It is therefore important that you should understand the sources of these authorities and the relationship between them.

It may be said that there are three main sources of employment law in this country:

Statute

The law directly enacted by the UK Parliament. It may take two forms: an Act of Parliament, e.g. **Employment Rights Act 1996, Equality Act 2010**; or a Statutory Instrument, brought into effect by an individual Minister under the authority of an enabling Act, e.g. **Working Time Regulations** (SI 1998/1833). Both of these forms of legislation are, of course, directly enforceable in the UK courts, and may be equally relied upon.

Case Law

Although over the past 30 years employment law has become dominated by statute, case law is still very important. Not only does case law both interpret the statute and "fill in the gaps" between statutes, but certain areas of employment law are still heavily dependent upon the common law, e.g. claims for wrongful dismissal.

An example of case law interpreting legislation would be: **The Race Relations Act 1976** (now the Equality Act 2010 s.9(1)(c)) referred to "ethnic origin", the case of *Mandla v Dowell Lee* [1983] I.C.R. 385 HL laid down a test to interpret this term and determine the conditions to be met by a group wishing to bring itself within the protection of the (now) Equality Act. Consequently, if you were asked in an examination to consider whether discrimination in an employment context against, say, an inhabitant of the Isle of Wight was unlawful, you would need to consider first the statute itself and then the subsequent case law in arriving at your answer.

European Law

It is outside the scope of this book to consider the detail of the legislative process of the EU, but there are several issues you will need to remember:

(a) EU law is supreme over national law. In any conflict between the two, European law will take precedence.

(b) Many Treaty Articles have been shown to be directly effective, both vertically (may be relied upon in a national court by an individual against the state) and horizontally (may be relied upon in a national court by an individual against another individual).

Of particular importance in employment law is art.157, which states that men and women should receive equal pay for equal work. Article 157 (at that time, art.141) was held to be directly effective by the ECJ in the case of *Defrenne v Sabena* (case 43/75).

(c) A Directive is an instruction to a Member State to adapt its law to conform to EU requirements.

A Directive may have direct effect if it is sufficiently clear and precise, but may only be relied upon by an individual in a national court against the state or an emanation of the state; in other words a Directive may have vertical direct effect only.

(d) The ECJ plays a very important part in the UK judicial system, in particular in the field of employment law. Questions on points of EU law may be referred to the ECJ by any national court. The decision or opinion of the ECJ will in practice be binding on the national court, both in the instant case and also as precedent for future cases (although you should remember that the ECJ itself is not bound by its own previous decisions). Consequently, decisions of the ECJ referring to cases within other Member States of the EU will also form precedents for UK national courts.

QUESTION AND ANSWER

The Question

"The impact of European Law into English Employment Law has been considerable, but problems have arisen in transposing the requirements of some Directives into national legislation." Discuss.

The scope of European intervention, from (say) Equal Pay, through (say) Health and Safety measures, to (say) Harassment.

Explanation of how European law (both legislation and case law) becomes part of national law.

Examples of incomplete transposition of Directives (e.g. omission of Work of Equal Value from original Equal Pay Act 1970, definition of harassment amended by 2008 Regulations and now within the Equality Act 2010).

Role of the courts in "policing" such issues.

The Tribunal and Court System

Employment Tribunals (previously known as Industrial Tribunals) have jurisdiction to hear almost all individual disputes based on statutory employment law claims and, in addition, common law contract claims arising from or outstanding at the termination of employment up to a maximum of £25,000.

An Employment Tribunal is normally comprised of three members: an ET judge, usually a barrister or solicitor of at least seven years' standing; and two lay members, drawn from either side of industry, one having had experience as perhaps a trade union official, the other having had management or trade association experience. Although it is uncommon, it is possible for the lay members to outvote the legally qualified chair. In certain circumstances the chairperson, renamed "employment judge" by the Employment Tribunals Act 1996 s.3A, may sit alone to hear claims.

The tribunal system was set up with the aims that it should be quicker, cheaper, more efficient and more accessible than the normal court system. In much of this it has been successful, although delays are not now uncommon partly due to the increased number of claims being made, and also partly due to the increased use of legal representation, particularly by employers, which tends to slow the system down.

There are a number of advantages and disadvantages to the tribunal system, and these include:

(a) Informality, lack of ceremony, regalia, etc. Hearings are normally conducted in a room, which although perhaps purpose built, is very similar to any meeting or small function room.

(b) Representation may be by the party themselves, a lawyer, a trade union representative, a friend, etc., although it should be noted that most companies tend to be legally represented.

(c) Legal Aid is not available for first instance tribunal hearings, but may be available for appeal hearings before the Employment Appeals Tribunal (EAT).

(d) Costs are rarely awarded, thus there is little financial threat to an applicant wishing to bring a claim.

(e) The members of the tribunal are specialist and experienced in employment disputes. Unlike magistrates or most judges, members of an employment tribunal hear only cases within one area of law.

(f) Certain rules of evidence, e.g. hearsay, do not apply.

At the time of writing it has been proposed by the government that a fee should be introduced, payable by the applicant before a tribunal hearing may be brought, consequently (d) above may need to be modified.

The procedure for bringing a complaint before an Employment Tribunal is fairly straightforward. The applicant completes a form and sends it to the tribunal office. A copy of the form is then sent to the employer who has 14 days in which to respond. Both the original form and the employer's response are then copied and sent to the Advisory Conciliation and Arbitration Service (ACAS), who may then attempt to obtain a settlement between the parties. If the claim is not settled at this stage, the tribunal will then make a preliminary examination of the case and may hold a pre-hearing review, often consisting of a tribunal judge sitting alone; this is in order to "weed out" particularly weak cases. Once a case goes to a full tribunal hearing the procedure adopted is similar in many ways to a court hearing; normally open to the public, it is basically an adversarial procedure, with each party putting its case, witnesses may be called and examined, other evidence introduced. However, unlike judges in most court hearings, the members of the tribunal take a much more active role in proceedings, questioning the parties and, if appropriate, leading applicants through the hearing procedure.

It is now standard practice for the tribunal to give the reasons for its decision in summary form, rather than in extended form, although this does not apply to cases of equal pay or discrimination.

If the applicant's claim is successful, the tribunal may award any of three remedies: reinstatement, re-engagement or compensation. Perhaps not surprisingly, the most often awarded remedy is compensation—although when the tribunal system was first introduced it was thought that reinstatement or re-engagement would be the most commonly sought remedies.

An appeal against a decision of an Employment Tribunal on a point of law only may be made to the EAT. The EAT has the similar standing and many of the same powers as the High Court, and an appeal from the EAT goes to the Court of Appeal, and on occasion from there to the Supreme Court (previously the House of Lords).

The Employment Tribunal is bound by the decisions of the EAT and other superior courts; the EAT, whilst its own previous decisions are only persuasive, is bound by decisions of the Court of Appeal and the Supreme Court.

Figure 1 Court and Tribunal System

You should now know and understand:

- the basic tribunal and court system regarding employment law.

QUESTION AND ANSWER

The Question

"The tribunal system was designed to afford rapid and easy access to justice for members of the public. In that respect it has not been completely successful." Discuss.

Suggested points for consideration

Aims of the system—speed, efficiency, self-representation, lack of formalities etc.

Problems encountered—number of claims, shortage of funding, increased legal representation by companies, complexity of legal issues, apparent inconsistencies of judgments in some areas, etc.

"Solutions" introduced—increased legislation, statutory procedures (e.g. the now discontinued dispute resolution etc.), restriction of appeals from ET to EAT, judges sitting alone to hear certain issues, recent extension of jurisdiction, suggestions to impose a fee on applications, etc.

Who is an Employee?

Employment law governs the relationship between the employer and the employee. Employers and employees have various rights, duties and liabilities to and for each other in law.

An employer may have vicarious liability for the actions of his employees in the course of their employment; an employer has a duty to deduct income tax and National Insurance contributions from an employee's wages; an employer owes a particular standard of care to his employees in regard to Health and Safety; and an employer is bound by the terms and conditions of the contract of employment. Likewise, an employee is also bound by the contract of employment; an employee has the right not to be unfairly dismissed by his employer; in many circumstances an employee has the right to redundancy payments, the right to statutory notice periods, statutory holidays and statutory time off, etc.

It is therefore essential to be able to identify "an employee", and differentiate between employees and self-employed workers, sometimes called "independent contractors", who are generally not covered by the same laws and rules.

LEGISLATION HIGHLIGHTER

EMPLOYMENT RIGHTS ACT 1996 SECTION 203

DEFINITIONS AND TESTS

Statutory definition

Often it is not difficult to identify an employee. Section 230(1) Employment Rights Act 1996 (ERA) states, "In this Act 'employee' means an individual who has entered into or works under ... a contract of employment." The Act goes on to state in s.230(2), "In this Act 'contract of employment' means a contract of service or apprenticeship, whether express or implied, and (if it is express) whether oral or in writing."

Problems do sometimes arise though in differentiating between employees and self-employed workers; whereas employees work under a contract of employment or a contract of service, a self-employed worker, or independent contractor, works under a contract for services.

It is not always easy to distinguish between the two, as for instance in the following brief examples:

(a) A sales representative who works exclusively for a company from their offices, but supplies his own car and is paid gross, without deduction of tax or NI.

(b) An accounts clerk who has worked from home on a part-time basis for a company over a number of years.

(c) A part-time lecturer who regularly works for two or more universities during each academic year.

At this point it may be helpful to consider separately the approach of the courts when dealing with, on the one hand, typical workers (those who work perhaps a standard number of hours per week and/or on a regular basis), and, on the other hand, atypical workers (those who work on a casual or non-regular basis).

TYPICAL WORKERS

Over the years the courts have developed and applied various tests in an effort to formally determine who is an employee.

The Control Test
Formulated in the case of *Yewens v Noakes* (1880) 6 QB 530 by Bramwell L.J., where he stated, "A servant is a person subject to the command of his master as to the manner in which he shall do his work." However, as working practices have changed over the years, and as industry has become more technical and required more specialist expertise, it has become obvious that the control test alone will not suffice. As Cooke J. stated in the case of *Market Investigations v Minister of Social Security* [1969] 2 QB 173, "control will no doubt always have to be considered, although it can no longer be regarded as the sole determining factor."

The Integration Test
Proposed and adopted by Denning L.J. from *Cassidy v Ministry of Health* [1951] 2 KB 353 and applied in *Stevenson Jordan & Harrison v MacDonald and Evans* [1952] T.L.R. 101, the integration test asked whether the worker's work is an integral part of the business; if so, the worker is an employee. If the worker's work is merely accessory to the business, then the worker is an independent contractor. The problem with the test is that it appears to call for

a value judgment by the court without explaining the steps necessary in arriving at that judgment. Perhaps not surprisingly the test found little favour generally.

Multiple or Economic Reality Test

Proposed in the case of *Ready Mixed Concrete (South East) Ltd v Minister of Pensions & National Insurance* [1968] 2 QB 497 by McKenna J., it asked three questions: first, did the servant agree to provide his work in consideration of a wage or other remuneration; second, did he agree, either expressly or impliedly, to be subject to the other's control to a sufficient degree to make the other master; and third, are the other provisions of the contract consistent with it being a contract of service.

McKenna J. also pointed out that "a man does not cease to run a business on his own account because he agrees to run it efficiently or to accept another's superintendence." This test, in conjunction with the "business test" (below), has been strengthened by the House of Lords' ruling in *Carmichael v National Power Plc* [1999] I.C.R. 1226, in which it was stated that before a finding of employee status could be found, there must be (a) a sufficiency of control, and (b) contractual mutuality of obligation. Thus the RMC test may be read as:

(a) does a contract exist governing the working relationship between the parties;

(b) is there sufficient control by the company over the worker; and

(c) are the other provisions of the contract consistent with it being a contract of employment.

KEY CASE

CARMICHAEL V NATIONAL POWER PLC [1999] 4 ALL E.R. 897

Mrs Carmichael worked as a guide for National Power on a "casual as required" basis, showing groups of visitors around Blythe power station. She worked some hours most weeks for a number of years. She wore a company uniform, was sometimes provided with a company vehicle, and enjoyed many of the benefits of full-time employees. The question for the court to determine was whether there was an on-going "umbrella" or "global" employment contract covering both the periods which she worked and the intervening times.

Held: (HL) During those periods Mrs Carmichael was not actually ful-filling her duties she was not an employee. For an on-going contract of employment to exist there must be both a sufficiency of control and mutuality of obligation. The mutuality of obligation—the obligation on the part of the company to provide work, and on the part of the worker to accept the work offered—must be contractual in nature, rather than merely a moral obligation.

Commentary

This decision reinforces the approach taken in *O'Kelly* (supra), and makes clear that for the finding of employee status there must, as an irreducible minimum, be both a sufficiency of control and contractual mutuality of obligation.

The Business Test

In many ways, this test is an extension of the Multiple or Economic Reality Test. It was formulated in the case of *Market Investigations v Minister of Social Security* [1969] 2 QB 173 by Cooke J. and asks the fundamental question "is the worker in business on their own account?" It then considers such factors as control; whether the worker provides his own equipment; whether he hires his own helpers; what degree of financial risk he runs; whether the worker has responsibility for investment and management of the work; and what, if any, opportunity the worker has to profit from the sound management of the task. In the later case of *Lee Ting Sang v Chung Chi-Keung* [1990] I.R.L.R. 236, the Privy Council stated that whilst there was no single test for determining employment status, the standard to be applied was best stated by the test from Market Investigations.

Other Approaches

In the mid-1990s the courts appear to have adopted a somewhat different approach, rather than applying formalistic tests, there are several instances of the courts taking a more holistic or, at times, a more pragmatic, approach. In the case of *Hall (HM Inspector of Taxes) v Lorimer* [1994] I.R.L.R. 171, a case concerning income tax assessment on either Sch.D or Sch.E basis, the court warned against the application of "mechanical tests", and took the view that each case should be decided on its own facts. In that case, the number of different companies the respondent had worked for and the short duration of each engagement were important factors—although they were not factors specifically considered in previous tests—in enabling the court to find that Mr Lorimer was self-employed.

In *Lane v Shire Roofing Co (Oxford) Ltd* [1995] I.R.L.R. 493, the facts of which showed similarities with several earlier cases, the Court of Appeal, whilst referring with approval to the line of authority and various tests defining employment status, were at pains to point out that the facts must be viewed and any tests applied with reference to modern working practices. In this case involving personal injury, Mr Lane was found to be an employee.

It should, however, be noted that, following the case of *Carmichael*, it is difficult to see how such approaches may be justified today.

. . . .

OTHER ISSUES

On the topic of employee status, a number of other issues need to be considered.

Substitution

In both the *RMC* Case and the later case of *Express & Echo Publications Ltd v Tanton* [1999] I.R.L.R. 367 the courts have been influenced in their decisions by the power of the worker to provide a substitute, rather than undertake the work himself. In view of the personal nature of the employment contract, courts have accepted that if the worker has the authority to provide a substitute to do the work on their behalf, it is very unlikely that the worker's contract will be a contract of employment. However in the case of *McFarlane v Glasgow City Council* [2001] I.R.L.R. 7 the court held that a substitution clause which could only be exercised by the worker with the approval of the employer may not be sufficient to deny employee status, approved and extended in *Autoclenz v Belcher* [2011] UKSC 41.

Self-Description

Even if the parties themselves agree on the employment status of the worker, this may by no means be conclusive to the courts. In the case of *Ferguson v John Dawson & Partners (Contractors) Ltd* [1976] 3 All E.R. 817, even when the worker gave a false name, presumably in order to avoid payment of tax, and both parties had agreed that he was employed on a self-employed basis, the court by a majority decision still held that the company was his employer and that he was working under a contract of employment. As Browne L.J. stated: "The parties cannot by a label decide the true nature of their relationship".

Ferguson is often discussed in conjunction with the later case of *Massey v Crown Life Insurance Co* [1978] I.C.R. 590, in which a manager took professional advice and decided to change his employment status, with agreement from his employer, from employee to self-employed for tax reasons. Some two years later Mr Massey was dismissed and wished to claim for unfair dismissal—an option which was only open to him if he was held to be an employee. Based on the decision in Ferguson, it perhaps appeared that he had a strong case to succeed. However, the court held that he was self-employed, Lord Denning M.R. famously stating, "Having made his bed as being self-employed, he must lie on it".

The two decisions appear to conflict, although the cases on their facts appear somewhat similar. They may, however, perhaps be reconciled.

Ferguson concerned a labourer who, in order to obtain work, joined a company on the basis on which they hired—a supposed self-employed, independent contractor status ("the lump")—he himself having little say in the matter. Massey concerned a senior employee who took professional advice and chose to change his status for his own financial advantage. The major difference between the cases, however, is the reason that they came before the courts; Ferguson concerning liability for personal injury, and Massey for a claim for unfair dismissal compensation. The courts often appear more willing to find employee status in favour of the applicant in cases concerning injury, than in those which involve tax or dismissal claims.

In a recent EAT decision (*Levy McCallum Ltd v Middleton EAT Judgment*, August 9, 2005, unreported), Serota J. stated the preferred position: "If parties agree to create a horse but instead create a camel, the fact that they intended to create a horse and even call what they have created a horse is of little assistance in determining whether it is in fact a horse".

Fact or Law?

The Court of Appeal in the case of *O'Kelly v Trusthouse Forte Plc* [1983] 3 All E.R. 456 stated that it had for over 70 years been established law that the employment status of an individual was a question of fact, rather than a question of law. This was reiterated by the Privy Council in *Lee Ting Sang v Chung Chi-Keung* [1990] I.R.L.R. 236. The significance of this is that an appellate court should not interfere with a finding of fact, unless to use the words of Lord Simonds in *Edwards v Bairstow* [1956] AC 14 the trial court took "a view of the facts which could not reasonably be entertained". In other words, it is generally not possible to appeal against a finding of fact.

On occasion however the question of employment status may turn solely on the examination and interpretation of a document, as was the case in *The President of the Methodist Conference v Parfitt* [1984] I.R.L.R. 141. In such a case, the Court of Appeal ruled, the question would become a question of law, and an appellate court would thus have jurisdiction to interfere if necessary.

ATYPICAL WORKERS

Agency Workers and Casual Workers

The status of "agency workers", "casual workers" or "temps" is still in many cases unresolved.

The case of *Wickens v Champion Employment* [1984] I.C.R. 365 suggested that agency workers were not employees, since the "relationship between the employers and temporaries seems to us wholly to lack the elements of continuity, and care of the employer for the employee, that one associates with a contract of service". Nevertheless, the Court of Appeal in *McMeechan v Secretary of State for Employment* [1997] I.R.L.R. 353 held that a temporary worker can have the status of employee of the employment agency in respect of each individual assignment worked, and this is supported by the Court of Appeal in the case of *Clark v Oxfordshire Health Authority* [1998] I.R.L.R. 125.

However, the later case of *Montgomery v Johnson Underwood Ltd* [2001] I.C.R. 819 casts doubt on this reasoning. The Court of Appeal, following the House of Lords in *Carmichael*, pointed out that both control and mutuality of obligation must be present before a contract of employment can be identified. In the case of agency workers, although mutuality of obligation may exist between the agency and the worker, control over the worker is exercised on a day-to-day basis not by the agency but by the client company. Thus, it is argued, agency workers will apparently not be employees of either the agency or the client company. The court suggested that they may have a contract *sui generis*, since in most cases it is obvious that the worker is not a genuine self-employed independent contractor.

The issue has since been examined by the Court of Appeal in the case of *Dacas v Brook Street Bureau(UK) Ltd* [2004] I.R.L.R. 358 where it was held that there was neither sufficient mutuality of obligation nor sufficient control between the agency and the worker to satisfy the requirements of Carmichael, thus reinforcing the position that agency and other casual workers are unlikely to be able to prove employee status.

Many of the problems concerning the status of agency workers have now been addressed by the **Agency Workers Regulations 2010** (SI 2010/93) implementing Directive 2008/104/EC, granting agency workers who have completed 12 weeks continual work with the end-user the same rights and status as workers permanently employed by that end-user.

James v London Borough of Greenwich [2008] IRLR 302

Ms James worked for Greenwich Council from September 2001 as a Housing Support Worker, her services being provided via an employment agency. In 2003 she changed agencies. The agreement between Ms James and the agency described her as self-employed and stated that she worked on a "contract of services" not a contract of employment.

During her time with the council she was subject to day-to-day control by the council consistent with the existence of a contract of employment. She was provided with necessary materials and issued with a staff badge; however, she was not entitled to sick pay or holiday pay from the council, nor did the council's disciplinary and grievance procedures apply to her.

In 2004 she was absent from work due to illness. On her return she found that she had been replaced by the agency and her services were no longer required. She complained of unfair dismissal, and as a preliminary issue the tribunal needed to consider her employment status.

Held: The Court of Appeal held that the EAT were entitled on the facts to find that no contract, either express or implied, existed between Ms James and the council. There was no mutuality of obligation between those parties sufficient to satisfy the requirements of the Carmichael case. Importantly, the court stated that a contract of employment should not be implied into a relationship unless it was necessary to do so in order to explain the relationship; in this case the relationship between the worker and the council was explained by the presence of the contracts between the council and the agency, and the agency and Ms James.

Commentary

This case restricts the approach taken by courts in cases such as *Harlow DC v O'Mahony* (UKEAT/0144/07) and *National Grid Electricity Transmission v Wood* (UKEAT/0432/07) in which the courts were not reluctant to find an implied contract of employment between the "agency worker" and the "end user". The approach in *James* has recently been adopted in *Tilson v Alstrom Transport* [2010] EWCA Civ 1308.

Mutuality of Obligation

This "test" has been used on a number of occasions, particularly to try to determine the status of part-time, casual or "agency" workers.

It was used in the case of *O'Kelly v Trusthouse Forte Plc* [1983] 3 All E.R. 456 to prove that part-time casual catering workers were not employees, since the court found that the company were under no obligation to provide work, and the workers were under no obligation to accept work if it were offered.

The importance of this factor was confirmed by the House of Lords in the case of *Carmichael v National Power Plc* [1999] I.C.R. 1226 who made clear that both control and mutuality of obligation are essential features of a contract of employment. Moreover, the test for mutuality of obligation must be applied in a contractual manner; in other words, the worker must be under a contractual obligation to accept work and the company under a contractual obligation to offer it. An attempt by the Court of Appeal in *Carmichael* [1998] I.R.L.R. 30 to mollify the test by introducing the element of reasonableness was firmly rejected by the House of Lords.

A rather different approach was adopted in the earlier case of *Nethermere (St Neots) Ltd v Taverna and Gardiner* [1984] I.R.L.R. 240, a case concerning the employment status of outworkers or home workers. A similar test was applied to show that although mutuality of obligation as such did not exist, the existence of "well founded expectations of continuing home work" could, over the period of a year or more, give rise to the existence of a contract of employment. Thus the home workers were employees. It is difficult to predict how widely the courts may use this approach of "implying a contract of employment" (see *James v LB Greenwich* ante) based on "well founded expectations" of the parties; such an approach neither conforms to normal contractual principles, nor to the approach in *Carmichael*. A different approach was seen in *Cornwall CC v Prater* [2006] I.R.L.R. 362 in which the Court of Appeal found that in the case of a teacher employed by the council on a series of individual contracts, mutuality of obligation did exist during periods of work, and the periods between contracts were not sufficient to break continuity of employment (see also *Ford v Warwickshire CC* [1983] I.R.L.R. 126).

Illegal Contracts

It may be, particularly in cases of "self-description", that a court may find that a professed self-employed independent contractor is in fact an employee, working under a contract of employment, and that the reason for the "self-employed" label was to evade the payment of PAYE income tax – a criminal offence. In such cases the courts have on occasion found that the contract was illegal, and as such void; in which case no rights or obligations could arise under it (e.g. *Jennings v Westwood Engineering* [1975] IRLR 245). However, the Court of Appeal in the joined cases of *Enfield Technical Services v Payne: Grace v BF Components* [2008] IRLR 500 has held that a mere mislabelling of a contract is, in itself, not enough to make the contract illegal.

Figure 2

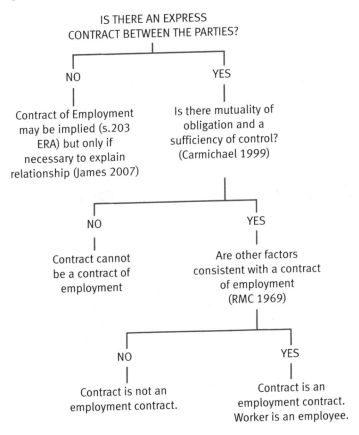

Chapter Checklist

You should now know and understand:

- why it is necessary to distinguish between a contract of service and a contract of employment;

- how the courts distinguish between an employee and an independent contractor.

QUESTION AND ANSWER

The Question

Adam is an insurance salesman with XCo Ltd. He has been an employee for over three years. He spends most of his time either working from home using a computer terminal supplied by the company, and visiting customers, using his own car, for which he is paid an allowance. On average Adam spends no more than half a day per week in the company's offices.

The company have recently suggested to Adam that he change his status from employee to self-employed, as they believe this will result in financial benefit to both parties.

Advise Adam.

Suggested points for consideration

A genuine change of Adam's status from employee to self-employed may well benefit both parties financially:

For Adam it would mean that he may offset various expenses against tax payable, almost certainly showing a financial benefit. However, he will lose many of the rights of an employee, e.g. redundancy payments, right to complain of unfair dismissal, etc.

For the company, not only will there be financial savings on payrolling and employer's NI contributions, etc., but their liability will be considerably decreased in many situations: no employer's vicarious liability, reduced standard of care in many situations, many employee's rights will not apply, e.g. redundancy, unfair dismissal, etc.

Would the courts accept such a change of status?

Consider the "multiple test" (*Ready Mix Concrete*).

Is Adam in business on his own account? (*Market Investigations*).

Self description (*Ferguson* cf. *Massey*).

Possible issue of illegality of the contract (*Jennings* cf *Enfield Technical Services*)

Reason for the court's involvement (*Lorimer* cf. *Lane*).

The Contract of Employment

In many respects the contract of employment is very similar to any other contract. Usually, a contract of employment will be expressed in writing, but as with many other contracts this need not always be the case. A statutory definition is given as "a contract of service or apprenticeship, whether express or implied, and (if it is express) whether oral or in writing." (s.230(2) of the ERA 1996).

LEGISLATION HIGHLIGHTER

EMPLOYMENT RIGHTS ACT SECTION 1

The contract of employment will consist of a number of terms and conditions. These may be either express terms or implied terms. Express terms are those terms which have been agreed between the parties, either orally or in writing. Implied terms are those which are so obvious to an onlooker that they are held to be part of the contract, and therefore do not need to be expressed by the parties. Many textbooks will include, among the implied terms, those imposed by statute.

Breach by either party of any of the terms of the contract will, of course, amount to a breach of contract; if the term is held to be a fundamental term of the contract, the breach would allow the injured party to treat the contract as terminated, and act accordingly.

EXPRESS TERMS

Under s.1 of the ERA 1996, every employer must give to each employee, within two months of the commencement of employment, a written statement of the particulars of employment. Failure to provide the statement within two months allows the employee to complain to an employment tribunal under s.11 of the ERA, and the tribunal may decide what particulars should be included.

This "s.1 statement" must include:
 (a) the names of the employer and employee;

(b) the date on which the employment began;

(c) the date on which the employee's period of continuous employment began, which would take into account any previous employment which counts as continuous;

(d) the scale and/or rate of remuneration;

(e) the intervals at which remuneration is paid;

(f) terms and conditions regarding hours of work;

(g) details regarding holidays and holiday pay;

(h) details regarding sickness/injury and sick pay (here the employee may be referred to separate document);

(i) pension and pension scheme provisions (here the employee may be referred to a separate document);

(j) notice periods;

(k) in the case of temporary positions, the length of contract or expected date of termination;

(l) place(s) of work;

(m) any collective agreements which may affect the terms and conditions of employment (these details may be provided in a separate document);

(n) a note concerning disciplinary rules and procedures (here the employee may be referred to a separate document)—this is not necessary where the total number of employees is less than 20;

(o) some further details must be given if the employee is to work outside the UK.

It is common practice for employers to include all of these details in a written contract of employment, which, once signed by the parties becomes legally binding. If the employer does not choose to do this, a separate s.1 statement must then be issued; such a statement would not in itself be a contract (unless signed as a contract by the parties (*Gascol Conversions Ltd v Mercer* [1974] I.C.R. 420), but would allow a tribunal to draw strong prima facie evidence of the contents of the employment contract (*System Floors (UK) Ltd v Daniel* [1982] I.C.R. 54).

Collective Bargaining

The results or products of collective bargaining may affect an individual's contract of employment by, in theory, any of three ways. The first and most obvious is by express incorporation into the contract. If a term is agreed upon by the parties whereby the, say, rate of pay is affected by the collective agreement in force between the trade union and the employer, the rate of pay to the employee may be varied accordingly without the need for any further agreement (*Robertson v British Gas* [1983] I.R.L.R. 302). Such a term may be included in the contracts of employment of both union members and non-union members.

The second theory of incorporation into an individual employee's contract is by way of agency—the idea that the trade union is acting as agent for its members as individuals. Although the laws of agency may permit this, in practice it is most unlikely that either the union or its members would wish to be so bound.

The case of *Burton Group v Smith* [1977] I.R.L.R. 351 is authority for the presumption that the trade union does not act as agent for its individual members in collective agreements.

Thirdly and finally, it may be possible to incorporate the products of collective agreements (or indeed many other terms) into an individual's contract by conduct; in effect as part of custom and practice (see below).

It is, of course, possible for almost any term to become an express term of the contract, if agreed to by both parties.

It appears that the Unfair Contract Terms Act 1977 does not apply to the contract of employment (*Commerzbank AG v Keen* [2007] I.R.L.R. 132, impliedly overruling dicta in *Johnstone v Bloomsbury Health Authority* [1992] QB 333 and *Brigden v American Express Bank* [2000] I.R.L.R. 94)—the contract may not be taken to operate with the employee as the consumer. It should also be noted that the wording of the Unfair Terms in Consumer Contracts Regulations 1999 specifically excludes employment contracts.

. . . .

IMPLIED TERMS

On the Part of the Employer
It is generally held that an employer must comply with four major implied terms: a duty to pay wages, a duty to exercise reasonable care, a duty to provide a grievance procedure, and a duty of mutual trust and confidence.

Duty to Pay Wages
Wages are the major consideration for the work done by the employee. Unless expressly agreed, wages may not be paid in kind, but must be paid as money. However, there is no implied right for an employee to be paid in cash; payment may be made by credit transfer to the employee's bank, by cheque or by wage packet, etc. Part II of the ERA 1996 protects employees from unauthorised deductions from wages. It does not, however, apply in the following situations:

(a) where the deduction is made under a statutory provision (s.13(1)(a) of the ERA 1996);

(b) where the deduction is made under a provision in the worker's contract of employment (s.13(1)(a) of the ERA 1996);

(c) where the worker has consented in writing to the deduction (s.13(1)(b) of the ERA 1996);

(d) where the deduction is the reimbursement for an overpayment in wages (s.14(1)(a) of the ERA 1996), although the deduction will normally only be permitted by the courts if the original overpayment was a mistake of fact (rather than a mistake of law), and even so the employer may be estopped from making the deduction if the employee had been led to believe the money to be his, had acted on that belief, and the overpayment had not been the fault of the employee (*Avon CC v Howlett* [1983] I.R.L.R. 171);

(e) an over-payment of work related expenses (s.14(1)(b) of the ERA 1996) subject to similar conditions as (d) above;

(f) where the deduction is made on account of the worker having taken part in a strike or other industrial action (s.14(5) of the ERA 1996), for application of this see the cases of *Miles v Wakefield MDC* [1987] I.R.L.R. 193 and *Wiluszynski v Tower Hamlets LBC* [1989] I.C.R. 493.

A failure to pay wages is held to constitute a deduction for the purpose of the ERA (*Delaney v Staples t/a De Montfort Recruitment* [1992] 1 A.C. 687), but a failure to pay monies in lieu of notice is not. Money in lieu of notice is traditionally held to be damages for wrongful dismissal, and not wages (*Delaney v Staples*). Be aware, however, of the decision in *EMI v Coldicott* [1999] I.R.L.R. 630, where it was held that if the payment of money in lieu of notice is made under authorisation of an express term of the employment contract, the money will be taken to be remuneration arising from the contract rather than being damages for breach of contract—as such, of course, the money will be liable to taxation.

If the issue of sick pay is not covered by an express term of the contract, the courts have held that there is no presumption of a right to wages when off sick; each case will be considered on its merits (*Mears v Safecar Security Ltd* [1960] QB 54).

Generally there is no obligation on the part of the employer to provide work, as long as wages are paid (*Collier v Sunday Referee Publishing Co Ltd* [1940] 2 KB 647), but the courts have identified two main areas where the employer may be under a duty to provide work:

(a) where payment is made on a commission or piecework basis (*Devonald v Rosser & Sons Ltd* [1906] 2 KB 728);

(b) where an employee is engaged on skilled work and needs to continue to work to maintain or develop that level of skill (*Breach v Epsylon Industries Ltd* [1976] I.C.R. 316), or where publicity or public exposure is understood to form part of the consideration due to the employee, e.g. an entertainer, actor, etc. (*Turner v Sawdon & Co* [1901] 2 KB 653).

Additionally, if the contract provides, either expressly or impliedly, that the work will be provided, failure by the employer to do so would amount to an actionable breach (*William Hill Organisation Ltd v Tucker* [1998] I.R.L.R. 313).

Duty to Exercise Reasonable Care.

At common law, the employer is under a duty to take reasonable care for the health and safety of his employees. The standard of care is "the care which an ordinary prudent employer would take in all the circumstances" (*Paris v Stepney BC* [1951] 1 All E.R. 42). This duty is owed to employees as individuals (*Paris v Stepney BC*), and consequently a higher standard of duty may be owed to some employees than to others (*James v Hepworth & Grandage Ltd* [1968] 1 QB 94)—see also chapter "Health and Safety". The employer should provide safe plant and premises, a safe system of work and reasonably competent fellow employees.

Duty to Provide a Grievance Procedure.

The employer has a duty to both provide and effectively operate a grievance procedure (*WA Goold (Pearmak) Ltd v McConnell* [1995] I.R.L.R. 516). In the case of *Bracebridge Engineering Ltd v Darby* [1990] I.R.L.R. 3 it was held that failure to investigate or take seriously a complaint of sexual harassment constituted a fundamental breach of contract.

Duty of Mutual Trust and Confidence.

Sometimes also referred to as a duty to cooperate, or the duty of mutual cooperation. The duty has been defined by the court as an obligation on the employer that he should not "without reasonable and proper cause, conduct [himself] in a manner calculated to, or likely to, destroy or seriously damage the relationship of confidence and trust between employer and employee" (*Woods v WM Car Services (Peterborough) Ltd* [1981] I.C.R. 666.

Cases to illustrate a breach of this duty include:
(a) *Isle of Wight Tourist Board v Coombes* [1976] I.R.L.R. 413, where a manager said of his secretary that she was an "intolerable bitch on a Monday morning."
(b) *Post Office v Roberts* [1980] I.R.L.R. 347, where a senior manager wrote an unfavourable report on an employee without consideration of her work record, which resulted in her being refused promotion.

(c) *Malik v BCCI* [1997] I.R.L.R. 462, where the dishonest conduct of the employer may amount to a breach of mutual trust and confidence.

It should, of course, be remembered that conduct that may be acceptable in one particular industry or situation, may not be acceptable in another, and in those circumstances may be held to amount to a breach of the duty of trust and confidence. In recent years the courts have both widened the scope and increased the importance of the implied term of mutual trust and confidence (see e.g. "constructive dismissal"). The case of *University of Nottingham v Eyett* [1998] I.R.L.R. 646 suggests that, although in previous cases the duty of trust and confidence has been expressed in a negative form, i.e. refraining from conduct likely to harm the relationship, in principle the duty may have a positive form, and in appropriate cases may be breached by a failure on the part of the employer to warn or act.

The issue of mutual trust and confidence is often linked with issues of dismissal. Whilst the common law remedy for any breach of contractual term will normally be damages (the amount of which is determined by the court and limited only by common law principles), if the breach is part of the dismissal process the remedy will form part of the statutory compensation available for unfair dismissal (the amount of which is limited by statute) For examples of the application of these rules see the cases of *Johnson v Unisys* [2001] I.R.L.R. 279, *Eastwood v Magnox* [2005] 1 AC 503, *Dunnachie v Kingston upon Hull CC* [2004] I.R.L.R. 727.

On the Part of the Employee

The employee is also bound by a number of implied terms; these are generally held to be a duty of obedience, a duty to adapt, a duty to exercise care and a duty of fidelity or good faith.

Duty of Obedience

An employee has a duty to obey all reasonable and lawful orders. The employer may not, however, order the employee to do an illegal act (*Morrish v Henlys (Folkestone) Ltd* [1973] I.C.R. 482), nor may the employer order the employee into immediate danger (*Ottoman Bank v Chakarian* [1930] A.C. 277).

Duty to Adapt

Generally an employee has a duty to adapt to new methods and techniques introduced by the employer, in such cases though, the employer should provide appropriate training or retraining (*Cresswell v Board of Inland Revenue* [1984] I.C.R. 508).

In each case the court must decide whether the changes amount to merely an adaptation of the way in which the job is carried out, or a change of the job itself, in which case the question of redundancy may arise (*North Riding Garages Ltd v Butterwick* [1967] 2 QB 56).

Employees must also have to adapt to unilaterally imposed changes to terms and conditions if an express term allowing the employer to change or amend other terms is contained within the contract (see e.g. *Bateman v ASDA Ltd* [2010] IRLR 370), providing that such changes and the manner of making such changes do not breach the duty of mutual trust and confidence.

Duty to Exercise Care

The employee has a general duty to exercise reasonable care in the performance of his work.

The practical importance of this usually arises in an action in tort where the employee has acted negligently causing injury to a third party, and the employer is held vicariously liable for the employee's actions. In such a situation the employer may be able to sue the employee for an indemnity, either for breach of contract (*Lister v Romford Ice and Cold Storage Co Ltd* [1957] A.C. 555), or in tort, where both are held to be joint tortfeasors, for either a contribution or a full indemnity. It should be noted that both such actions are extremely rare, and in effect, are contrary to the notion of employer's vicarious liability.

Duty of Fidelity or Good Faith

The courts have held that virtually any act by the employee which is inconsistent with the contract of employment and which does or may cause injury to the employer will amount to a breach by the employee of the duty of fidelity or good faith.

This duty may be broken down into several sub-headings:
(a) duty to account for secret profits made by the employee in the course of his employment (*Boston Deep Sea Fishing and Ice Co v Ansell*).
(b) duty not to compete with the employer whilst in employment (*Hivac Ltd v Park Royal Scientific Instruments Ltd* [1946] ch.169), although the courts are reluctant to place any unnecessary restrictions on an individual's spare time.
(c) duty regarding competition by ex-employees. With the exception of an express contract term restraining an employee from competition after leaving the employment and a general protection of trade secrets (see "Restraint of Trade"), it may be difficult to show a duty of fidelity regarding an employee's actions following the termination of the contract of employment (although see the Australian case of *Ansell Rubber Co v Allied Rubber Industries* [1967] V.R. 37). Many actions which would constitute a breach of the duty of fidelity if carried out by an employee,

may be quite lawful if carried out by an ex-employee. Thus, most breaches of this duty are actually committed by employees prior to leaving his employment either to join another company or to set up business on his own.

Examples of this include:

Wessex Dairies Ltd v Smith [1935] 2 KB 80, canvassing his employer's customers prior to setting up his own business.

Robb v Green [1895] 2 QB 315, making or memorising a list of the employer's customers prior to setting up his own business.

(d) duty to co-operate. In the cases of both *Secretary of State for Employment v ASLEF* (no.2) [1972] 2 QB 455 and *Ticehurst v British Telecommunications Plc* [1992] I.R.L.R. 219 the courts have held that actions taken by employees with the intention of disrupting the employer's business may amount to a breach of contract; even though that action may be no more than a "work to rule", which by its very nature means working to the terms of the contract but no further.

Work Rules

Although the contract of employment will contain either an express or an implied term that the employee will abide by "the rules", unless individually specified in the contract, these rules may not have contractual force in themselves (*Secretary of State for Employment v ASLEF* (no.2) [1972] 2 QB 455).

One effect of this is very much in favour of the employer, in that, although breach of the rules by the employee may be a breach of the contract term of duty to obey orders, since the rules themselves do not have contractual force, the employer may change them unilaterally without breaching the contract—subject of course to constraints of "mutual trust and confidence".

Custom and Practice

In reality, there is very little significance or importance today in the incorporation of terms into the contract of employment through custom and practice. For a term to be incorporated through custom and practice it should be notorious, certain and reasonable. The leading case is *Sagar v H Ridehalgh & Son Ltd* [1931] 1 ch.310.

Statute

The growth of statute as a source of employment law over the past few years has had considerable impact on the contract of employment. There are perhaps three ways in which statute may affect the actual contract terms:

(a) On occasion statute directly imposes a term into the contract of employment, e.g. the Equality Act 2010 s.66 imposes an equality clause into all contracts of employment.

(b) Statute may often operate to restrict or negative a contract term, e.g. provisions within the Equality Act would make void any contract term which purported to restrict promotion prospects for women.

(c) Whilst breach by the employer of statute will normally be actionable by the employee in its own right, it may also amount to a breach of the duty of mutual trust and confidence.

KEY CASE

UNITED BANK LTD V AKHTAR [1989] I.R.L.R. 507
A junior bank employee, whose contract contained an express mobility clause, was instructed to move from Leeds to the Birmingham offices of his employers, at only six days' notice and with no financial assistance. He refused, partly due to family circumstances, left the company, and claimed unfair dismissal owing to his having been constructively dismissed.

Held: Despite the express mobility clause in the employment contract, the employee had been constructively dismissed, since, the EAT held, it was necessary to imply into the contract a requirement that the employer should not exercise a term in such a way that the employee was unable to comply with it.

Commentary
This decision, although undoubtedly fair on the facts, comes dangerously close to reintroducing the "reasonableness test", specifically rejected by the Court of Appeal in *Western Excavating*. A better way of looking at the decision would perhaps be to confirm that the employer was not in breach of contract by enforcing a contractual term, but that the way in which a term was invoked could breach the implied term of mutual trust and confidence. The breach of this implied term may then give grounds for constructive dismissal.

DRYDEN V GREATER GLASGOW HEALTH BOARD [1992] I.R.L.R. 469

Ms Dryden was employed as a nursing auxiliary in a Glasgow hospital. She smoked approximately 30 cigarettes per day. Due to the nature of her job, she was unable to leave the premises during the working day, but until 1991 areas had been set aside inside the hospital where smoking was permitted.

In 1991, following consultation, a policy was implemented banning smoking in all general and maternity hospitals. All staff were given notice of the change, and offered advice and counselling. 10 days after the policy was implemented Ms Dryden resigned and claimed she had been constructively dismissed.

Held: Dismissing her claim, the EAT stated that there was no implied term that an employee was permitted to smoke at work, nor had the employers acted in such a way so as to prevent the employee from carrying out her part of the contract, therefore they had not breached the duty of mutual trust and confidence.

An employer is entitled to make rules for the conduct of their employees, and if a rule is introduced for a legitimate purpose, the fact that it bears hard on a particular employee does not in itself lead to a breach of contract.

Commentary

Two issues may be considered. Firstly, Ms Dryden had worked at the hospital for some 14 years, during all of which time she had smoked with the implied permission of her employer. It was not, however, fully argued whether a "right to smoke" may have been implied into her employment contract through either conduct or custom and practice. Secondly, it may be that the tribunal was influenced by the fact that Ms Dryden's place of work was a maternity hospital.

Figure 3 Contract of Employment

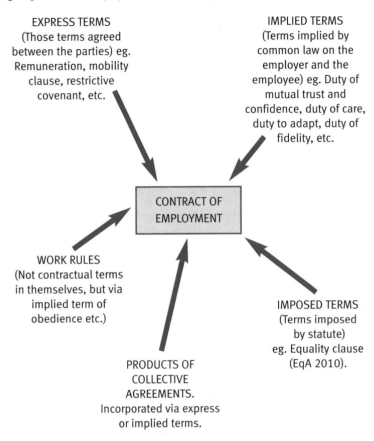

EXPRESS TERMS
(Those terms agreed
between the parties) eg.
Remuneration, mobility
clause, restrictive
covenant, etc.

IMPLIED TERMS
(Terms implied by
common law on the
employer and the
employee) eg. Duty of
mutual trust and
confidence, duty of care,
duty to adapt, duty of
fidelity, etc.

CONTRACT OF
EMPLOYMENT

WORK RULES
(Not contractual terms
in themselves, but via
implied term of
obedience etc.)

IMPOSED TERMS
(Terms imposed
by statute)
eg. Equality clause
(EqA 2010).

PRODUCTS OF
COLLECTIVE
AGREEMENTS.
Incorporated via express
or implied terms.

You should now know and understand:

- the legal status of a Section 1 statement;
- how terms become incorporated into the contract of employment;
- how an employer may enforce a contractual term;
- the importance and scope of the term of mutual trust and confidence.

QUESTION AND ANSWER

The Question

Clive has worked as a laboratory technician for XCo Ltd since 2000 at their Manchester works.

In January 2005, Clive was sent a revised statement of terms and conditions which contained among other things the following clause: "The company reserves the right to transfer any employee either temporarily or permanently to any of the company's business premises anywhere within the UK." As requested, Clive signed and returned the bottom copy of the document to the personnel office.

Last week Clive was informed by the personnel manager that owing to a downturn in work at the Manchester offices Clive would be transferred next month to the Birmingham branch.

Clive complained that this would entail either relocation or considerable daily travel, neither of which was acceptable. The personnel manager referred Clive to the mobility clause, and told him: "You have no option; work in Birmingham or resign."

Advise Clive.

Suggested points for consideration

In advising Clive, the first thing to consider is whether the mobility clause contained in the January 2005 statement forms part of his contract of employment (*Gascol Conversions*). If it does, then the company have every contractual right to enforce it (*Western Excavating*), as long as it is not invoked in such a way so as to breach the duty of mutual trust and confidence (*United Bank*). (Consider, perhaps, whether cases such as *High Table v Horst* may be of assistance to Clive.)

If the mobility clause does not form part of the employment contract, the company would have to rely on an implied mobility clause under the terms of mutual trust and confidence and the employee's duty of co-operation, but it is very unlikely on the facts of Clive's case that such an argument would succeed (*Aparau v Iceland Frozen Foods*).

The other issue here concerns the words used by the personnel manager. If Clive leaves the company, has there been a dismissal, which there must be for a successful redundancy or unfair dismissal claim. Is this a case of resignation under the threat of dismissal (*Sussex CC v Walker*), or would the employer's actions constitute a repudiatory breach of the contract in which case s.95(1)(c) of the ERA 1996 would apply?

Equality of Treatment

The Equality Act 2010 covers and has replaced the Equal Pay Act 1970, the Sex Discrimination Act 1975, the Race Relations Act 1976, the Disability Discrimination Act 1995, and secondary legislation covering discrimination on the grounds of Age, Religion or Belief, Sexual Orientation, and Gender Reassignment.

At the time of writing there is very little authoritative caselaw on the Equality Act 2010, but it is possible to use existing caselaw generated under the old statutes to explain and demonstrate the workings of the new legislation.

The Equality Act covers the conduct of the employer during the recruitment process, the employment relationship, and the time after that relationship has ended.

The legislation is overseen by the Commission for Equality and Human Rights (CEHR). It was formed in 2007 to take over from the Equal Opportunities Commission (EOC), the Commission for Racial Equality (CRE) and the Disability Rights Commission (DRC)

The EOC was set up under the Sex Discrimination Act 1975, and the CRE under the Race Relations Act 1976. Both had powers under the relevant Act to conduct formal investigations, to issue non- discrimination notices, to act in the case of discriminatory advertisements, to seek injunction through the civil courts to restrain persistent offenders, and to assist individuals in bringing actions. In 1999, the DRC was formed under the Disability Discrimination Act to perform a similar function to the EOC and CRE. All three commissions were charged with reviewing and recommending on policy and legislative issues. The scope of the CEHR is somewhat wider and also covers discrimination on the grounds of age, sexual orientation or religion or belief, along with the remit to encourage good practice in human rights generally.

KEY STATUTE

Equality Act 2010

Equality of Terms: Equal Pay

Equal pay legislation in the UK is twofold: national legislation—the Equality Act 2010; and art.157 of the EU Treaty, along with the explanatory EU Directives nos 75/117 and 76/207.

In the case of *Pickstone v Freemans Plc* [1988] I.R.L.R. 357 the House of Lords stated that the national legislation must be interpreted purposively in line with the Treaty Article and Directive 75/117. Normally, therefore, a national court will have no need, nor authority, to consider EU provisions, if the national legislation provides a full and adequate remedy (*Blaik v Post Office* [1994] I.R.L.R. 280).

The Equality Act 2010 ch3.

It is possible for a woman or a man to bring a claim for equal pay under any of three heads within the Equality Act. In each case it is necessary that the applicant selects a comparator, who must be of the opposite sex. The choice of comparator is for the applicant to make (*Picksone v Freemans Plc*), but may not be a hypothetical comparator although it may be a predecessor (*Macarthys Ltd v Smith* [1980] I.C.R. 672) but not a successor (the earlier case of *Diocese of Hallam Trustee v Connaughton* [1996] I.R.L.R. 505 was held to have been wrongly decided by the EAT in *Walton Neurological Centre v Bewley* [2008] IRLR 505). The applicant may choose either a single comparator or multiple comparators (*Hayward v Cammell Laird Shipbuilders* [1988] I.C.R. 464). If the applicant is unable to name a comparator, they may be granted discovery to enable them to obtain sufficient details—however such discovery may not be used as a "fishing trip" permitting an applicant to trawl through personnel records in search of likely comparators, etc. (*Leverton v Clwyd CC* [1989] I.C.R. 33). It is also necessary that both the applicant and the comparator(s) are employed either by the same employer at the same establishment, or by the same or associated employer at an establishment at which "common terms and conditions of employment are observed" (*Leverton v Clwyd CC*). The House of Lords in *British Coal Corp v Smith* [1996] I.R.L.R. 404 took a broad approach to this, stating that it was sufficient that the terms should be "substantially comparable." On the issue of choice of comparators, it is worth considering the case of *South Ayrshire Council v Morton* [2002] I.R.L.R. 256, which permitted employees of one Local Education Authority to choose as comparators employees of another Local Education Authority, and which may extend the range available to certain applicants; although be aware of the Court of Appeal decision in *Robertson v Department of Environment, Food and Rural Affairs* [2005] IRLR 363, in which it was held that members of one government department may not use members of a different government department as comparators, since each government department has the authority to agree many of the terms and conditions of its civil servants. It would therefore appear that dicta from such as *Lawrence v Regent Office Care Ltd* [2002] I.R.L.R. 822 and *South Ayrshire v Morton* will only be relevant to situations involving authorities controlled by a particular government department, and that cross-departmental claims, and almost certainly similar private sector claims, will be excluded. It is, however, clear that different types of employees, e.g. "white collar" workers and manual workers, may be used as comparators, providing the employer is a "single source" (*City of Edinburgh v Wilkinson* [2010] IRLR 756).

The three heads of claim are: like work, work rated as equivalent, and work of equal value.

Like Work

Section 65 Equality Act 2010 states that an applicant may bring a claim if the work they do is "the same" as or of "a broadly similar nature" to the work done by their chosen comparator; and the work will be of a broadly similar nature if any differences are of no practical importance. In the case of *Capper Pass Ltd v Lawton* [1977] I.C.R. 83, the EAT adopted a "broad brush approach" in holding that the work done by the applicant, the directors' cook, was sufficiently similar to the work done by cooks in the works canteen for the claim to succeed.

Likewise, in the case of *Shields v E Coombes (Holdings) Ltd* [1978] I.C.R. 1159 where male counterhands were paid more than females since, according to the employer, the males acted not only "as a deterrent to attack ... or other trouble" but also to deal with any such trouble until the police arrived, the Court of Appeal held that since in the previous three years there had been no such trouble, the additional responsibilities of the males were of no practical importance. Consequently, the applicant's claim succeeded.

However, in cases where differences relate to genuine differences in levels of responsibility or consequences of mistakes, these differences may be sufficient to defeat a claim (*Eaton Ltd v Nuttall* [1977] I.C.R. 272).

A three stage approach was set out by Bridge L.J. in *Shields v Coombes* for claims based on like work:

> "First, was their work of the same or a broadly similar nature? Second, if so, were any differences between the things she did and the things he did (regard being had to the frequency, nature and extent of such differences) of practical importance ... Third ... Can the employer then prove that any variation between the woman's contract and the man's is genuinely due to a material difference (other than the difference of sex) between her case and his?"

Work Rated as Equivalent

If a job evaluation study has been carried out and agreed by the parties (*Arnold v Beecham Group* [1982] I.R.L.R. 307), it may be relied upon to found a claim for equal pay. The job evaluation study must, of course, be objective (*Rummler v Dato-Druck GmbH* [1987] I.C.R. 774).

Work of Equal Value

Section 65 of the Equality Act states:

"A's work is of equal value to B's work if it is –

(a) Neither like B's work nor rated as equivalent to B's work, but

(b) Nevertheless equal to B's work in terms of the demands made on A by reference to factors such as effort, skill and decision-making."

It is for the applicant to choose under which head they wish to bring their claim, although they must consider whether a claim under "like work" would be more appropriate; they may wish to claim under "equal value" even if, prima facie, there is an available comparator to enable a claim under "like work" (*Pickstone v Freemans Plc*). This prevents the employer from employing a token male on like work and so avoiding the purpose of the legislation.

The procedure involved in an equal value claim is as follows. Once the claim has been brought to the tribunal, the tribunal must consider whether there are, prima facie, reasonable grounds for determining that the work is of equal value. If so, the tribunal may commission an independent expert to carry out a study   tribunal would then adjourn while the expert report is prepared. Although it is usual for the tribunal to accept the expert's report in full, it does not have to. There are occasions where a part of the report have been ignored (*Wells v F Smales & Sons Ltd* (1985) 281 I.R.L.I.B. 11), or where the report's conclusion has been rejected entirely (*Tennants Textile Colours Ltd v Todd* [1989] I.R.L.R. 3).

Material Factor Defence

A claim may be defeated if the employer can show that the difference in terms is due to a material factor, reliance on which "does not involve treating A less favourable because of A's sex that the (employer) treats B, and if the factor is within subsection (2), is a proportionate means of achieving a legitimate aim". Subsection (2) states that a "factor is within this subsection if A shows that, as a result of the factor, A and persons of the same sex doing equal work to A's are put at a particular disadvantage when compared with persons of the opposite sex doing work equal to A's".

Those material factors which refer specifically to the individual worker will not normally present any problems to the tribunal. It is quite acceptable that factors such as length of service, seniority, responsibility or qualifications may be acceptable as defences.

However, problems may arise with factors which are due to the operation of the employer's business or more general market factors. It is worth considering some of these in some detail:

(a) Red-circling, where an internal reorganisation reduces the grade of some workers but allows them to retain their previous salary scale. If the red-circling is discriminatory or has been brought about by some past discrimination it will not be permitted as a valid defence (*Snoxell v Vauxhall Motors Ltd* [1977] I.C.R. 700). In any event, red-circling should not exist any longer than is necessary.

(b) Collective agreements may be accepted as defences, but they must be genuinely operated, transparent in classification systems and not tainted by any discriminatory attitudes. It is for the employer to rebut any suggestions of discrimination and explain how any job evaluation study worked (see *Rummler v Dato-Druck* GmbH Case 237/85 [1986] E.C.R. 2101, *Danfoss Case* 109/88 [1989] I.R.L.R. 532).

(c) Performance related pay, commission based, piecework or target related. It is for the employer to show objective justification for any pay differences between men and women, in much the same way as for collective agreements (*Royal Copenhagen Case* C-400/93 [1995] I.R.L.R. 648).

(d) Part-time working. Traditionally most part-time workers have been women, thus discrimination against part-timers is indirect discrimination against women, and will be, prima facie, unlawful. However, discrimination in fringe pay, e.g. overtime and shift allowances may be permissible if it can be objectively justified (*Calder v Rowntree Mackintosh Confectionary Ltd* [1993] I.R.L.R. 212).

(e) Market forces. At first glance, it would appear that a "market forces" defence should succeed. If a company is able to attract a class or group of people to work for less than others it would make sound financial sense to do so. However, considering the inequalities of bargaining power in employment and the fact that traditionally men have been able to command higher wages than women, to allow such a carte blanche defence would obviously seriously undermine both domestic and EU legislation.

The approach of the courts is demonstrated in the following cases:

(a) *Rainey v Greater Glasgow Health Board* [1987] I.C.R. 129, the House of Lords held that market forces may constitute a defence if they amounted to a genuine, objective reason. Although this decision has been criticised, it may be justified if viewed as a form of red-circling, particularly if viewed in the light of the following case.

(b) *Benveniste v University of Southampton* [1989] I.R.L.R. 122, where the court held that market forces could only amount to a genuine material factor defence for as long as those particular facts existed. Once the market or financial constraints eased, the defence would no longer be available.

(c) *Enderby v Frenchay Health Authority* [1994] I.C.R. 112, in which the ECJ stated that it was "for the national court to determine, if necessary by applying the principle of proportionality, whether and to what extent the shortage of candidates for a job and the need to attract them by higher pay constitutes an objectively justified economic ground for the difference in pay..."

(d) *Ratcliffe v North Yorkshire CC* [1995] I.R.L.R. 439 where the House of Lords held that the employer could not cut the wages of employees in order to compete with an external contractor for a competitive tender, thus denying a market forces defence.

KEY CASE

GLASGOW CITY COUNCIL V MARSHALL [2000] I.R.L.R. 272

There were eight applicants in the case, seven female and one male. All were instructors in special schools in Scotland and claimed equal pay with teachers working in the same schools. The female instructors named a male teacher as comparator and the male instructor named a female teacher. It was accepted that although teachers had higher qualifications than the instructors, both groups performed the same or broadly similar work. It was therefore for the employers to establish a defence, which they did by arguing both that the pay structure was the result of collective negotiations, and also by introducing statistical evidence to show that the pay structures did not discriminate on the grounds of gender.

Held: The claim would fail since all instructors, both male and female, were paid the same "instructor" rate as agreed by collective bargaining, and all teachers, whether male or female were paid at the same agreed "teacher" rate—thus, differences in pay were not the result of discrimination on the grounds of sex.

The House of Lords laid down a four stage approach:
 (i) The explanation for differences in pay must be genuine.

(ii) As a question of causation, the less favourable treatment complained of is due to the reason given in that explanation.

(iii) The reason is not the difference of sex, either directly or indirectly.

(iv) The factor relied upon is a material difference between the woman's case and the man's case.

Commentary

As Lord Slynn stated: "This is plainly in essence a claim that the pay is not fair; and not a claim that the pay is unequal because of discrimination between the sexes. As such, it does not fall within the Equal Pay Act 1970."

KEY CASE

HAYWARD V CAMMELL LAIRD SHIPBUILDERS [1988] I.C.R. 464

Ms Hayward, who was employed as a cook, brought a claim for equal pay, by claiming that her work was of equal value with that of male painters, joiners and insulation fitters employed by the same company.

Held: Her claim succeeded. Furthermore, it was held that the individual components of the pay packages of Ms Hayward and her comparators should be equalised, not just the overall total.

Commentary

This is a useful case, since it is good authority for several propositions: an applicant may choose their own comparator; an applicant may choose multiple comparators if they wish; individual components of pay should be compared and equalised, not just the overall package; the supposed danger of "leap-frogging" does not constitute a defence; and finally, it is the first case of an equal value claim brought in this country.

Figure 4 Equality of Terms

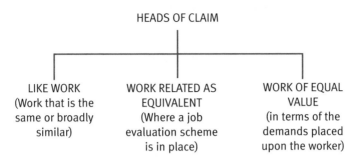

HEADS OF CLAIM

| LIKE WORK (Work that is the same or broadly similar) | WORK RELATED AS EQUIVALENT (Where a job evaluation scheme is in place) | WORK OF EQUAL VALUE (in terms of the demands placed upon the worker) |

Chapter Checklist

You should now know and understand:

- the three heads of claim for equality of terms;

- issues regarding the choice of comparator;

- the role of the independent expert;

- defences available to the employer.

QUESTION AND ANSWER

The Question

David and Emily are employed as machine operators by XCo. David has worked for them for one and a half years, and Emily for eight months.

Emily discovers that David earns £12.00 per hour, whereas she is only paid £10.50 per hour. She also discovers that fork lift truck drivers employed by a subsidiary of XCo in London are paid £13.00 per hour.

Advise XCo of the defences that may be available to them should Emily bring an equal pay claim.

Suggested points for consideration

Emily may bring two possible claims:
(a) A claim under like work, using David as her comparator; or
(b) A claim for work of equal value, using the fork lift operators as comparators.

The choice of comparators is for Emily to make (*Pickstone*), and she may choose multiple comparators if she wishes (*Hayward v Cammell Laird*).

Defences available to the company under a like work claim may include:

a) David has been employed for over twice as long as Emily, the pay difference may be justified if the company can show that it is part of a recognised pay structure that is not based on the sex of the employee.

b) If the company can show that David's pay has been "red circled" (*Snoxell*)

c) If there are material factors relevant to the work that David and Emily actually do (*Shields v Coombes*).

Factors which may defeat a claim for work of equal value include:

a) If the fork lift operators are women, Emily may not use them as comparators.

b) If the work of the fork lift operators is not of equal value to Emily's.

c) If common terms and conditions are not observed between XCo and their subsidiary (*Leverton*).

d) If the differential is due to different geographical locations (*NAAFI v Varley*).

Discrimination

At a basic level, "discrimination" means nothing more than choice. However, in an employment context the word has taken on a rather different meaning, and is used in a somewhat negative sense.

LEGISLATION HIGHLIGHTER

EQUALITY ACT 2010

In employment, it is, prima facie, unlawful to discriminate against an employee or potential employee on the grounds age, disability, gender reassignment, marriage and civil partnership, pregnancy and maternity, race, religion or belief, sex, and sexual orientation.

Some legislative protection is given to those with criminal records, under the **Rehabilitation of Offenders Act 1974**.

SCOPE OF THE LEGISLATION

The Equality Act 2010 applies equally to applicants for employment, employees, ex-employees, contract workers and self-employed workers providing a personal service to the employer.

THE PROTECTED CHARACTERISTICS

AGE DISCRIMINATION

Section 5 states that in relation to the protected characteristic of age:
"A reference to a person who has a particular protected characteristic is a reference to a person of a particular age group.

A reference to persons who share a protected characteristic is a reference to persons of the same age group."

The legislation covering age discrimination includes direct

discrimination (s.25(1)(a), s.13)—although it will amount to a defence if it can be shown that the treatment is a proportionate means of achieving a legitimate end (s.13(2)), indirect discrimination if the treatment cannot be shown to be a proportionate means of achieving a legitimate aim (s.25(1)(b), s.19), and harassment (s.26).

DISABILITY DISCRIMINATION

Disability is defined as being a physical or mental impairment which has a substantial and long-term adverse effect on the ability to carry out normal day-to-day activities (S6 (1)) See for example *Vicary v British Telecommunications Plc* [1999] I.R.L.R. 680 and *Ekpe v Metropolitan Police Commisioner* [2001] I.R.L.R. 605.

Progressive conditions such as cancer or HIV infection are now treated as amounting to a disability (Sch.1), as are severe disfigurements, although there is no definition of "severe".

Section 15 states that a person (A) discriminates against a disabled person (B) if, either, A treats B unfavourably because of something arising in consequence of B's disability, and A cannot show that the treatment is a proportionate means of achieving a legitimate aim. Two issues should be noted from the above wording, firstly, that there would appear to be considerable flexibility for interpretation of "arising in consequence", and secondly that the legislation does not require the use of a comparator.

Sections 20 and 21 of the Equality Act impose on an employer a duty to make reasonable adjustments to such things as premises, equipment, allocation of duties, working hours, time off, instructions, etc. Failure to make such adjustments amounts to discrimination.

As yet, there is very limited case law to fully interpret all the aspects of the law in this area. However, the following may be instructive:

An employer should plan ahead and consider the needs of future disabled employees (*Williams v Channel 5 Engg Services Ltd* case 230136/97).

It may be unlawful to select an applicant for redundancy on account of their disability, even where the employer takes the view that they must retain the most flexible workforce in order to meet their obligations (*Morse v Wiltshire CC* [1998] I.R.L.R. 352).

The duty to make adjustments does not extend to a duty to provide a carer for a disabled employee (*Kenny v Hampshire Constabulary* [1999] I.C.R. 27).

The duty to make adjustments may only arise once an employer knows or could reasonably know of the worker's disability (*O'Neill v Symm & Co Ltd*

[1998] I.R.L.R. 233), this issue is now covered by s.15(2) and consequently the case of *HJ Heinz Co Ltd v Kenrick* [2000] I.R.L.R. 144 should not be relied upon.

GENDER REASSIGNMENT

Section 7 states that a person has the protected characteristic of gender reassignment if the person is proposing to undergo, is undergoing or has undergone a process (or part of a process) for the purpose of reassigning the person's sex by changing physiological or other attributes of sex. This section also includes reference to a transsexual person.

The legislation (s.16) prohibits an employer from treating a person less favourably in relation to an absence if that absence is because of gender reassignment, or if the absence is for some other reason and it is not reasonable for the person to be treated less favourably. Indirect discrimination and harassment are also covered.

MARRIAGE AND CIVIL PARTNERSHIPS

The protection under the Act applies only to those who are married or in a civil partnership; it does not therefore apply to those who are single, divorced or living together, nor would it apply to any third party. Marriage and civil partnership is not a recognised characteristic in regard to harassment, but is a recognised characteristic in relation to direct discrimination (s.13(4)) and indirect discrimination (s.19).

PREGNANCY AND MATERNITY

Section 18 concerns discrimination against women because of pregnancy (s.16(2)(a)), illness as a result of pregnancy during the protected period (s.16(2)(b)), because she is on compulsory maternity leave (s.16(3)), because she is exercising or seeking to exercise, or has exercised or has sought to exercise, the right to ordinary or additional maternity leave (s.16(4)).

Issues may arise in terms of pregnancy related illness; it would appear that statute covers all pregnancy related illness which manifests itself during the pregnancy or maternity leave periods for perhaps as long as such illness persists. However, pregnancy related illnesses which do not manifest themselves until after the leave period has expired may not be covered, and would therefore be treated as any other illness (see *Brown v Rentokil* [1997]

IRLR 445, *Caledonia Bureau Investment and Property Ltd v Caffrey* [1998] IRLR 110).

A woman dismissed because of pregnancy or childbirth will also have the right to claim unfair dismissal. However, unfair dismissal compensation is statutorily capped, whereas there is no such upper limit on compensation for discrimination.

RACE DISCRIMINATION

The prohibition of discrimination on the grounds of race covers direct discrimination, indirect discrimination and harassment.

Section 9 defines "race" as including colour, nationality, and ethnic or national origins. It also includes racial groups which consist of two or more distinct racial groups, e.g. black British.

There is much case law to define more precisely the term "ethnic origin." The House of Lords in the case of *Mandla v Dowell Lee* [1983] I.R.L.R. 209 laid down a number of conditions to be considered for any group wishing to bring themselves within the protection of the Act:

(a) a long shared history, of which the group is conscious as distinguishing itself from other groups, and the memory of which it keeps alive; and

(b) a cultural tradition of its own, including family and social customs and manners, often but not necessarily associated with religious observance.

Both of these the House of Lords held to be essential.

(c) a common geographical origin or descent from a small number of common ancestors;

(d) a common language, that need not be exclusive to the group;

(e) a common literature;

(f) a common religion, different from neighbouring or surrounding groups;

(g) being a minority or oppressed or dominant group within a community.

These five conditions were held by the House of Lords to be important factors, but not essential.

Applying this "test" it was held in *Mandla v Dowell Lee* that Sikhs are an ethnic group.

Subsequent case law has decided the following:

(a) Jews are an ethnic group *Seide v Gillette Industries* [1980] I.R.L.R. 427)

(b) Gypsies are an ethnic group *CRE v Dutton* [1989] I.R.L.R. 8)

(c) Rastafarians are not an ethnic group *Dawkins v Dept of the Environment* [1993] I.R.L.R. 284)

(d) Jehovah's Witnesses are not an ethnic or racial group *Lovell-Badge v Norwich City College* case 1502237/97)

(e) The Race Relations Act (now the Equality Act s.9) covers the Welsh (*Gwynedd CC v Jones* [1986] I.C.R. 833)

(f) Both the Scots and the English are covered by the Race Relations Act (now the Equality Act s.9) by reference to "national origins" but not by "ethnic origins" *Northern Joint Police Board v Power* [1997], *Boyce v British Airways* [1997])

It should be noted that Sikhs, Jews, Jehovah's Witnesses and Rastafarians are also now protected on the grounds of religion or belief.

RELIGION OR BELIEF DISCRIMINATION

The Equality Act 2010 s.10 makes it unlawful in an employment context to discriminate by way of direct discrimination, indirect discrimination, victimisation or harassment based on the religion, religious belief or similar philosophical belief. The statute applies to potential employees, employees, contract workers, those undertaking vocational training and ex-employees. The employer will have liability for anything done relevant to these regulations by any employee, whether such action is with or without the employer's knowledge or approval, if it is carried out "in the course of employment." There is as yet relatively little authoritative case law in the area of religion or belief; one of the first EAT decisions on this issue was the case of *Azmi v Kirklees MBC* [2007] All E.R. 484 in which the court held that the local authority was justified in not permitting a Moslem teaching assistant to wear a full-face veil whilst teaching, as the rule applied to all teaching staff and was necessary on the grounds of proper communication between teaching staff and students.

The conduct complained of need not be directly related to the employee's own religion or beliefs; in *Saini v All Saints Haque Centre* [2009] IRLR 74 an employee successfully brought a claim when he was required to assist in the dismissal of a fellow employee on religious grounds.

The words "religion or belief" have been widely defined: the explanatory notes in the statute give examples such as Jainism, Zoroastrianism, Rastafarianism along with the more "mainstream" religions; the courts have held that druidism, pacifism, scientology and veganism are also protected; and the Act itself makes clear that a lack of religion is also covered.

SEX DISCRIMINATION

Section 11 of the Act refers equality to men and women, the only exception being under s.13(6) no account is to be taken of special treatment afforded to a woman in connection with pregnancy or childbirth.

The discrimination may be direct, indirect or harassment.

SEXUAL ORIENTATION DISCRIMINATION

Section 12 applies to both men and women and means a person's sexual orientation towards persons of the same sex, persons of the opposite sex, or persons of either sex.

It therefore applies to gay, lesbian, heterosexual and bi-sexual persons.

DIRECT DISCRIMINATION

A person (A) discriminates against another (B) if, because of a protected characteristic, A treats B less favourably than A treats or would treat others. (s.13(1)).

Case law has defined this as the "but for" test—would the victim have been treated differently but for his/her sex or race? (*James v Eastleigh BC* [1990] I.R.L.R. 288)

The motive for the discrimination is irrelevant (*James v Eastleigh*), thus direct discrimination brought about by good intentions or even unintentionally is still discrimination for the purpose of the Act.

Segregation on racial grounds constitutes direct discrimination (s.13(5)), but allowing segregation to occur has, under previous legislation, been held not actionable (*Pel Ltd v Modgill* [1980] I.R.L.R. 142).

There is case law to suggest that the de minimis rule should apply to discrimination—that is, if the act complained of is trivial, it need not constitute actionable discrimination (*Peake v Automotive Products* [1978] QB 233), however in recent years the courts have been reluctant to accept, let alone extend, this principle in practice.

It is necessary for the complainant to show that they have been treated less favourably than others, thus a comparison must be drawn between the treatment afforded the complainant and the treatment afforded or the treatment that would have been afforded to others who do not share the complainant's protected characteristic; according to s.23(1) there must be no material difference between the circumstances relating to the complainants circumstances and those of the comparator (see e.g. *Shamoon v Chief Constable of the Royal Ulster Constabulary* [2003] ICR 337).

The legislation allows for "associated discrimination" claims to be brought, although not in the areas of marriage and civil partnership, or pregnancy and maternity. Associated discrimination occurs when an employer treats a worker less favourably because of the protected characteristic of another; the Act speaks of "a protected characteristic", not "his protected characteristic".

INDIRECT DISCRIMINATION

Section 19 defines indirect discrimination as:

A person (A) discriminates against another (B) if A applies a provision, criterion or practice which is discriminatory in relation to a relevant protected characteristic of B's.

For the above purposes a provision, criterion or practice is discriminatory in relation to a relevant protected characteristic of B's if—

(a) A applies, or would apply, it to persons with whom B does not share the characteristic,

(b) it puts, or would put, persons with whom B shares the characteristic at a particular disadvantage when compared with persons with whom B does not share it,

(c) it puts, or would put, B at that disadvantage, and

(d) A cannot show it to be a proportionate means of achieving a legitimate aim.

Examples of indirect discrimination have included:

Discrimination against part-time workers, the majority of whom are women (*R. v Secretary of State for Employment*, Ex p. EOC [1994] 2 W.L.R. 409, which resulted in the removal of hour thresholds for certain employment rights by SI 1995/31).

An age restriction "must be between 17–28" was indirectly discriminatory against women because of family commitments (*Price v Civil Service Commission* [1978] I.C.R. 27).

A rule that the successful candidate should not have young children was held to be indirectly discriminatory against women (*Thorndyke v Bell Fruit Ltd* [1979] I.R.L.R. 1).

A contractual requirement to work full-time may be indirectly discriminatory against women (*Home Office v Holmes* [1984] I.C.R. 678, although see the later case of *Greater Glasgow Health Board v Carey* [1987] I.R.L.R. 484).

The inclusion of a mobility clause in the employment contract may be discriminatory against women (*Meade-Hill v British Council* [1995] I.R.L.R. 478).

One problem that has arisen in cases of indirect discrimination has been the issue of the pool of comparators (see below *Jones v University of Manchester* [1993] ICR 474) but the wording of the present legislation should make much of the existing caselaw obsolete.

The Court of Appeal in *Jones v University of Manchester* [1993] I.C.R. 474 warned against sub-dividing or otherwise manipulating the pool in order to bring about a particular result. It held that the relevant pool is the number of persons referred to in the legislation, i.e. the number of persons to whom the requirement has been or would be applied to by the employer.

A defence provided by statute is for the employer to show that his action amounted to "a proportionate means of achieving a legitimate aim". In the case of *Hardy & Hansons Plc v Lax* [2005] I.R.L.R. 726 the Court of Appeal stated that "the principle of proportionality requires the tribunal to take into account the reasonable needs of the business. But it has to make its own judgment, upon a fair and detailed analysis of the working practices and business considerations involved, as to whether the (employer's) proposal is reasonably necessary." On this issue see e.g. *Azmi v Kirklees MBC* [2007] All ER 484, *Islington LBC v Ladele* [2009] ICR 387 etc.

Positive Discrimination

There is a difference between positive action and positive discrimination. Examples of positive action would be when an organisation seeks to promote applications for recruitment from certain, perhaps under-represented, sectors of society, e.g. ethnic minorities; or when a company actively encourages sections of its workforce, perhaps women, to attend training courses and seek promotions to positions in which they are under-represented. Such positive action is quite lawful, as long as the actual selection is made on merit and not on the basis of sex or origin.

Positive discrimination, for example restricting applications for a particular job to women only because women may be under-represented in that position or at that level, however, is generally not lawful. Discrimination in favour of one sex or any particular ethnic group will amount to discrimination against the other sex or other ethnic groups, and thus be contrary to the Equality Act.

However, art.2(4) of the **Equal Treatment Directive** allows for the introduction of "measures to promote equal opportunity for men and women, in particular by removing existing inequalities which affect women's opportunities." The ECJ have considered the extent to which this may allow positive discrimination, in a number of cases.

In the case of *Kalanke v Freie Hansestadt Bremen* [1995] I.R.L.R. 660 the court held that a rule which automatically gave priority to an equally qualified woman for a position in which women were under-represented, was contrary to the Equal Treatment Directive and would not fall within art.2(4) of the Directive.

In the later case of *Marschall v Land Nordrhein Westfalen* [1998] I.R.L.R. 39 the ECJ appear to have adopted a different approach, stating that such a rule may not breach the Equal Treatment Directive if there is a guarantee that all candidates will be subject to an objective assessment which takes into account all the factors specific to the individual candidate, and the criteria used in the assessment are not in themselves discriminatory. It may be argued that the reasoning in *Marschall* is, in itself, self-defeating; but it perhaps reflects a wider current European view that some positive discrimination in certain circumstances may not be harmful. In the later case of *Badeck's Application* [2000] I.R.L.R. 432, the ECJ allowed a scheme which assessed the suitability of applicants by taking into account issues such as experience of child care, but ignored factors such as partner's income, family responsibilities etc. Such a scheme would appear to work in favour of women, who in that case were the under-represented group, without offending against the Equal Treatment Directive. This may be compared to the scheme in *Abrahammsson v Fogelqvist* [2000] I.R.L.R. 732 which the ECJ found to be disproportionate to the aim pursued.

Harassment
Section 26 states:

"(1) A person (A) harasses another (B) if —
(a) A engages in unwanted conduct related to a relevant protected characteristic,
(b) and the conduct has the purpose or effect of
(i) violating B's dignity, or
(ii) creating an intimidating, hostile, degrading, humiliating or offensive environment for B,
(2) A also harasses B if—
(a) A engages in unwanted conduct of a sexual nature, and
(b) the conduct has the purpose or effect referred to in subsection (1)(b).
(3) A also harasses B if—
(a) A or another person engages in unwanted conduct of a sexual nature or that is related to gender reassingnment or sex,
(b) the conduct has the purpose or effect referred to in subsection (1)(b), and

(c) because of B's rejection of or submission to the conduct, A treats B less favourably than A would treat B if B had not rejected or submitted to the conduct.

(4) In deciding whether conduct has the effect referred to in subs.(1)(b), each of the following must be taken into account—

(a) the perception of B;

(b) the circumstances of the case;

(c) whether it is reasonable for the conduct to have that effect."

It is not yet clear how much relevance and weight the courts will place on existing case law when interpreting the new legislation, dicta in *Richmond Pharmacology v Dhaliwal* [2009] IRLR 336 suggests that prior caselaw is unlikely to be helpful, but it is likely that the two issues referred to below will be relevant:

(a) a single act, if sufficiently serious, may constitute harassment (*Bracebridge Engineering Ltd v Darby* [1990] I.R.L.R. 3)

(b) a single verbal comment, if sufficiently serious, may constitute harassment (*In Situ Cleaning Co Ltd v Heads* [1995] I.R.L.R. 4).

Bear in mind that if the harassment consists of a "course of conduct" action may be possible under the Protection from Harassment Act 1997 which creates both civil and criminal liability. The Court of Appeal ruling in *Majrowski v Guys and St Thomas' NHS Trust* [2005] I.R.L.R. 340 indicates that an employer may be vicariously liable under the Act for actions of their employees undertaken in the course of business. Although this Act was introduced primarily as "anti-stalking" legislation, there are some advantages to the victim in its use: it applies to any type of harassment, the limitation period is six years (unlike the three month period in discrimination law), and on occasion the award of damages may be wider.

Victimisation

Victimisation occurs when person A subjects person B to a detriment because B has done a protected act, or A believes that B has done or may do a protected act. Protected acts are defined by s.27 as bringing proceedings under the Equality Act, giving of evidence or information in connection with such proceedings, doing any other thing for the purpose of or in connection with the Act, or the making of an allegation that A or another person has contravened the Act.

It is therefore necessary for the complainant to show that a person who had not done the protected act would have been treated differently. For an example see the case of *Aziz v Trinity Street Taxis Ltd* [1988] I.C.R. 534. The later case of *Nagarajan v London Regional Transport* [1999] I.R.L.R. 572 makes it clear that it is not necessary that the respondent acted with the intention of victimising, it is sufficient that they did the act complained of and that the act was an important cause of the decision.

BURDEN OF PROOF

Section 136 states that once facts are presented from which the court could decide that a person has contravened the Act, the court must so decide unless the alleged contravener can show that they did not contravene the Act.

The effect is that it is no longer necessary for the complainant to prove their case, merely to establish the facts of the complaint. The burden of proof then moves to the person alleged to have discriminated, to rebut the presumption of discrimination. If they are not able to do so, the tribunal should then find discrimination.

Dress Codes
Whilst on the one hand the employer may issue rules regarding dress and uniform, and whilst these rules will normally form part of the work rules—breach of which may put an employee in breach of the employment contract—on the other hand, the rules themselves must not contravene discrimination laws.

In terms of sex discrimination, the courts have adopted the approach that dress rules will not normally breach discrimination law if they apply a similar standard of conventionality to both men and women (*Smith v Safeway Plc* [1996] I.R.L.R. 456).

Case law concerning racial discrimination is not quite so straightforward. Each case must be considered on its own facts and merits: in one case a ban on beards was not held to be unlawful discrimination against Sikhs (*Singh v Rowntree Mackintosh Ltd* [1979] I.R.L.R. 199), whereas in another case a Sikh woman dismissed for carrying a dagger contrary to the employer's work rules was unlawfully discriminated against (*Kaur v Butcher & Baker Foods Ltd* case 1304563/97).

Vicarious Liability
An employer may normally be held vicariously liable for acts committed by their employees in the course of their employment (s.109)

Under earlier case law, it was possible for an employer to avoid liability by arguing that it was no part of the employees job or duty to commit the acts complained of, and consequently, such acts were not committed in the course of employment (see *Irving v Post Office* [1987] I.R.L.R. 289).

However, the Court of Appeal in *Jones v Tower Boot Co Ltd* [1997] I.R.L.R. 168 rejected this approach, stating that the restrictive tortious definition of "in the course of employment" should not apply to cases of discrimination, but that the words should be given the broader definition a layman would apply to them. This purposive approach has been followed in the case of *Chief Constable of the Lincolnshire Police v Stubbs* [1999] I.R.L.R. 81, where the EAT held that, since work related social functions are an extension of employment, a male police officer who sexually harassed a female colleague at both an after work gathering and at an organised leaving party was acting "in the course of his employment" (but see also *Waters v Commissioner of Police for the Metropolis* [2000] IRLR 720).

The principles of vicarious liability in discrimination cases were extended by the EAT decision in *Burton and Rhule v De Vere Hotels* [1996] I.R.L.R. 596, in which it was held that an employer "subjects" an employee to the detriment of harassment when, in circumstances which he can control, he causes or permits the discrimination or harassment to take place—however, in *MacDonald* the House of Lords disapproved *Burton* on this issue, holding that an employer should only be liable for acts of their own employees, and not for actions of third parties. However, under s.40 an employer will be liable for harassment by a third party if they know that such harassment has taken place and fail to take reasonable steps to prevent an re-occurrence of such harassment.

Defences

It is a defence under Pt 1 Sch. 9 of the Act to a complaint of direct or indirect discrimination that the employer can show that there is an occupational requirement, and that the application of that requirement is a proportionate means of achieving a legitimate aim. The courts have tended to look at issues of occupational requirements strictly, examples include:

(a) the refusal to employ a female assistant in a menswear shop was held to be unlawful, since any intimate contact with customers could be undertaken by other male staff (*Wylie v Dee & Co (Menswear) Ltd* [1978] I.R.L.R. 103);

(b) the refusal to employ a male assistant in a women's dress shop was held to be unlawful, since any intimate contact with customers could have been performed by other female staff (*Etam Plc v Rowan* [1989] I.R.L.R. 150).

(c) the requirement that a post be filled by an Afro-Caribbean or someone of African descent at a play group where some 85 per cent of the children were from a similar ethnic background was upheld as a genuine occupational requirement (*Tottenham Green Under Fives Centre v Marshall* [1991] IRLR 162).

The best defence for an employer is that they have in place a comprehensive and effective equal opportunities policy—but such a policy must be properly promulgated and enforced among the workforce (*Balgobin v London Borough of Tower Hamlets* [1987] I.R.L.R. 401).

Remedies

Anyone who has suffered discrimination under the Act has the right to make a complaint to an employment tribunal within three months of the occurrence of the act complained of (s.123(1)(a)), but the tribunal has the power to extend the time limit if it considers that it is just and equitable to do so (s.123(1)(b)).

The usual remedy sought is one of compensation. Compensation is payable according to the principles applicable in tort and there is no upper limit to the amount of compensation that may be awarded. Compensation is not generally awarded against an employer in cases of unintentional indirect discrimination.

A further remedy lies within s.124, whereby the tribunal may make a recommendation that the respondent take within a specified period action to remove from the complainant the adverse effect of the discrimination complained of. Failure by the respondent to comply would allow the tribunal to increase or make an order for compensation.

In specific instances, further remedies may be available.

Chapter Checklist

You should now know and understand:

- the scope of the legislation concerning discrimination;

- the difference between direct and indirect discrimination;

- the difference between positive action and positive discrimination;

- the scope of the employer's liability;

- the defences available to an employer;

- the remedies available to a successful complainant.

QUESTION AND ANSWER

The Question

Felicity is 34 years old, a single mother with two young children, and has just started work for XCo Ltd on their production line. On her first morning she sees the production manager point at her and hears him ask the line supervisor: "Who's the new tart with the big knockers?"

Felicity is very upset by this remark, which she believes was overheard by several other workers; she goes to see the personnel manager to complain. He tells her "not to be a silly girl" and to return to work.

Advise Felicity.

Would your advice be different if Felicity also worked part time as an "exotic dancer" at the Blue Parrot Strip Club?

Suggested points for consideration

The question raises several issues:

(a) Does this situation fall within the definition of harassment.

(b) Even one remark, if sufficiently serious, can amount to sexual harassment (*In Situ Cleaning*), even if they were not addressed to Felicity (*De Souza v AA*).

(c) The company may be held vicariously liable for the actions of its employees, even if they were not sanctioned, if the actions were committed in the course of employment (*Jones v Tower Boot*).

(d) It is an implied term of the employment contract that it should have and operate an effective grievance procedure (*WA Goold (Pearmak) Ltd*), and in particular, failure by an employer to take seriously a complaint of sexual or racial discrimination will count heavily against the company (*In Situ Cleaning*).

Felicity may therefore be advised that she may have grounds to bring a complaint of direct sex discrimination against her employer, for which there is no requirement of any qualifying period of employment.

The relevance of Felicity being a part time exotic dancer is that the tribunal may take this and other details of the applicant's background and lifestyle into account when assessing the level of detriment suffered by her (*Wileman v Minilec Engg*) prior to awarding compensation.

Other Statutory Rights

7

. . . .

NATIONAL MINIMUM WAGE ACT 1998

The National Minimum Wage Act 1998 was introduced to provide a basic minimum hourly rate of pay for all workers. Section 2(1) enables the Secretary of State to determine and amend the hourly rate at appropriate intervals. Two rates of pay are set; one for workers aged 20 years and over, and a lower one for those workers aged 18–20 years. Under the 2004 National Minimum Wage Regulations 1999 (Amendment) Regulations, workers under 18 years of age who have left school are also afforded a statutory minimum wage.

Scope of the Act
The Act applies to all workers, not merely employees, and includes agency workers (s.34) and home workers (s.35)—but specific exclusions cover certain voluntary workers, members of the armed forces, prisoners and certain ship-board workers.

The National Minimum Wage Regulations 1999 apply also to situations where workers are permitted to sleep on the premises but are required to be available for work (see e.g. *South Manchester Abbeyfield Society v Hopkins* [2011] IRLR 300 cf. *Anderson v Jarvis Hotels* [2006] UKEAT 0062/05/3005).

Rights under the Act
The Act affords to all of those covered the right to be paid the minimum wage, the right of access to wage records, and the right not to suffer detriment for asserting a right under the Act—the remedy being via a complaint to an Employment Tribunal.

An employee who is dismissed for asserting a statutory right will be treated as having been unfairly dismissed (s.104 of the ERA 1996).

WORKING TIME REGULATIONS 1998

The Working Time Regulations are intended to implement the Working Time Directive 93/104/EC and parts of the Young Workers Directive 94/33/EC.

Main Provisions

A maximum working week of 48 hours, averaged over a 17-week period. It is possible for individuals to opt out of this restriction.

Night workers to average no more than eight hours work in each 24-hour period, calculated over a 17-week period. It is possible for individuals to opt out of this restriction.

Certain night workers—those involved with heavy physical or mental strain, or whose work involves particular special hazards—may work only eight hours in a 24-hour period, without exception.

All night workers are entitled to a health assessment before being required to work nights, and regular check-ups thereafter.

Adult workers are entitled to one day off per week, 11 continuous rest hours per day, and a minimum break of 20 minutes if the working day is six hours or more.

Young workers (those over the minimum school leaving age, but under 18 years old) are entitled to two days off per week, 12 continuous rest hours per day, and a minimum break of 30 minutes if the working day is four and a half hours or more.

All workers are entitled, after a 13 week qualifying period, to annual paid leave (the actual amount of holiday leave is periodically set by statutory instrument). Any provision within a contract claiming "there is no entitlement to paid holidays under this contract" have been held to be void (*The College of North East London v Leather*, EAT 30/11/01).

Holiday pay should normally be paid as a separate amount before or at the actual time of the holiday. Employers may pay holiday pay as a "rolled-up" figure (included in a total hourly, or similar, rate); but employers must ensure that such an arrangement is clearly notified to and agreed by the employee (*Marshalls Clay Products Ltd v Cauldfield* [2004] I.C.R. 436, and clarified by *Smith v AJ Morrisroes & Sons Ltd* [2005] I.R.L.R. 72).

"Worker" is defined in the Regulations in the same way as s.230(3) of the ERA, and includes both those working under a contract of employment (employees) and those working under any other contract to personally provide any work or service to another party, unless the other party's status under the contract is that of client or customer of any profession, or business undertaking, carried on by the individual.

The term "worker" also applies to apprentices, trainees and those on work experience programmes.

Almost certainly "worker" applies to casual workers, particularly following *Carmichael v National Power Plc* [1998] I.R.L.R. 301, but a Privy Council decision in *Chen Yuen v Royal Hong Kong Golf Club* [1998] I.C.R. 131 highlights an instance where, apparently and surprisingly, it was held that no contract of any sort was in existence between golf caddies and the golf club they "worked" for.

Agency workers are specifically included in the definition of "worker", by reg.36, the party responsible under the Regulations being the party who pays the agency worker—in most cases the employment agency.

Exclusions

Areas of activity excluded by the Regulations include:

Transport industry. Directive 2000/34 EC excludes mobile workers within the transport industry.

Junior doctors. Regulation 18(b) excludes all doctors under training.

Work at sea. Including fishing, shipping and offshore working.

Police and Armed Forces. The Regulations probably do not apply in most instances to ambulance service, fire service, prison service, etc.

Those with autonomous decision making powers as to the duration of their working time: for example, managing executives, those working in family businesses, etc.

Security work, requiring round-the-clock presence.

Continuous production processes, including hospitals, prisons, etc., although the exclusion is dependent upon the worker's activities, rather than merely on the place of work.

Seasonal industries, such as tourism, Christmas business, agricultural activities, e.g. fruit picking.

CASE EXAMPLE

BARBER V RJB MINING UK LTD [1999] I.R.L.R. 308
Pit deputies and colliery overmen at a privatised colliery were being required to work in excess of 48 hours per week. The employer argued that the men were only being asked to work their normal hours and the Working Time Directive was not to be read as forming part of the employment contract.

Held: The Directive, and by implication the Regulations, are a mandatory requirement and apply to all contracts of employment.

MATERNITY RIGHTS

Dismissal on Pregnancy-Related Grounds

An employee will be regarded as unfairly dismissed if the reason, or principal
reason, for her dismissal is that she is pregnant or any other reason connected with her pregnancy (s.99(1)(a) of the ERA 1996, and see by *Webb v
EMO Air Cargo* [1995] I.R.L.R. 645).

An employee will also be regarded as unfairly dismissed if during the
period of her maternity leave she submits a doctor's certificate stating that
due to illness she will be unable to return to work following the leave period,
and she is dismissed for a reason connected with the birth within four weeks
of the end of her maternity leave period (s.99(3) of the ERA 1996, and see
Brown v Rentokil Ltd [1997] I.R.L.R. 445).

It has been held that dismissal on the grounds of a pregnancy related
illness after the maternity leave ends may not constitute unfair dismissal
(*Hertz v Aldi Marked K/S* [1991] I.R.L.R. 31). However, be aware of the more
recent case of *Caledonia Bureau Investment & Property Ltd v Caffrey* [1998]
I.R.L.R. 110, in which it was held by the EAT that a dismissal, which occurred
after the maternity leave was over, for post-natal depression—a pregnancy
related illness—was for a reason connected with the pregnancy and therefore
contrary to s.99(1)—see also "Discrimination" above.

Maternity Leave

Legislation concerning provision of maternity leave is complex. Part VIII of the
ERA 1996, as amended by ERelA 1999 and the **Work and Families Act 2006**,
gives effect to the Pregnant Workers Directive (Directive 82/95) and now
provides for a minimum of 26 weeks' maternity leave to all pregnant
employees without the need for a minimum period of service, during which
time the employee should receive all rights under her contract of employment, except for wages or salary. In addition employees are entitled to 26
weeks of "additional maternity leave", during which contractual benefits are
restricted. Maternity leave may normally begin no earlier than the eleventh
week prior to the expected week of childbirth. During the maternity leave the
employee is entitled to all the normal benefits which would have accrued
under her contract, and, in the absence of any contractual right to pay, if she
has a minimum of 26 weeks of continuous service, is entitled to statutory
maternity pay.

She is normally entitled to return to work on terms no less favourable than she would have enjoyed had she not been absent.

Time Off for Ante-Natal Care
A pregnant employee has a right under s.55 of the ERA 1996 to time off during the employer's working hours to keep an appointment to receive ante-natal care.

KEY CASE

WEBB V EMO AIR CARGO (UK) LTD [1995] I.R.L.R. 645
Mrs Webb had been hired by EMO Air Cargo, a small company employing 16 people, as a replacement for one of their staff who was absent on maternity leave. It was envisaged that Mrs Webb would continue to work with EMO once the maternity replacement period was over. Some two weeks after starting work, Mrs Webb discovered that she was pregnant. On learning of this, her employer dismissed her. Mrs Webb brought a claim to an employment tribunal alleging sex discrimination.

Held: The House of Lords made the following points—

Discrimination on the grounds of pregnancy is sex discrimination. There is no need for the applicant to compare herself to a "sick man." It is possible that the dismissal may have been held to be a fair dismissal had Mrs Webb been appointed only on a fixed term contract (but see the case of *Carunana v Manchester Airport Plc* [1996] I.R.L.R. 378).

Commentary
Although a similar case today may be brought under s.99 of the ERA—dismissal on the grounds of pregnancy being automatically unfair—a sex discrimination claim may be advantageous because it would also cover the recruitment process, and also, unlike unfair dismissal claims, there is no upper limit on compensation awards for sex discrimination.

Parental Leave
The rights to parental leave are contained in the Maternity and Parental Leave Regulations 1999 as amended and allow parents with a minimum of one year's continuous service to take up to 13 weeks unpaid leave in respect of each child.

Paternity Leave

The EA 2002 makes provision for those employees with 26 weeks continuous service to be entitled to a period of at least two weeks paid paternity leave.

Adoption Leave

Under the EA 2002, provision is made for statutory adoption leave on a similar basis to the provision of paternity leave.

HUMAN RIGHTS ACT 1998

The Human Rights Act (HRA) 1998 has created new, directly enforceable rights against public bodies and against quasi-public bodies undertaking public functions.

The Act does not however make European Convention on Human Rights (the Convention) rights directly enforceable against a private litigant—an individual or a private business or company.

What the Act does is to give effect to Convention rights by obliging courts to decide all cases compatibly with Convention rights—unless prevented from doing so by primary legislation (s.6), by obliging courts wherever possible to interpret legislation in conformity with the Convention (s.3), and by requiring courts to take account of Convention based case law (s.2).

Generally, if legislation is held to be incompatible with the Convention, procedures are in place whereby the government can implement fast-track legislation to remedy the situation. Certainly in areas of criminal law, particularly evidential rules, the Act is likely to have considerable long-term impact (and see also issues of "right to strike" etc under Industrial Action).

PUBLIC INTEREST DISCLOSURE ACT 1998

The purpose of the Act is to protect workers against action taken by their employers in cases where the worker "blows the whistle" on certain actions of his employer.

The Act protects a worker against dismissal, selection for redundancy or any other detriment, if the reason or principal reason for the action is that the worker has made a "protected disclosure."

The term "worker" is given an extended definition by the Act and includes:
   (a) Those working under a contract of employment (s.230(3)(a) of the ERA 1996).
   (b) Those working under a contract to personally or otherwise provide any

work or services in a place that is not under the control of the individual—unless that other party is a client or customer of any profession or business carried out by the individual (i.e. unless the individual is genuinely running their own business) (s.230(3)(b) of the ERA 1996, as amended by PIDA).

(c) Agency workers, being those supplied or introduced by a third party (s.1 PIDA).

(d) A person providing medical, dental, ophthalmic or pharmaceutical services in accordance with arrangements made by a Health Authority under ss.29, 35, 38 or 41 of the **National Health Service Act 1977**, or the equivalent in Scotland (s.1 PIDA).

(e) A person being provided with training or work experience, unless under a contract of employment or as part of a course run by an educational establishment.

Qualifying Disclosure

A "qualifying disclosure" is defined in the Act as being a disclosure of information which the worker reasonably believes shows or tends to show:

(a) that a criminal offence has been, is being or is likely to be committed;

(b) that a person has failed, is failing or is likely to fail to comply with a legal obligation;

(c) that a miscarriage of justice has occurred, is occurring or is likely to occur;

(d) that health and safety has been, is being or is likely to be endangered;

(e) that the environment has been, is being or is likely to be damaged; or

(f) that information concerning any of the above has been, is being or is likely to be deliberately concealed.

It is immaterial whether the relevant failure occurs or would occur in the UK or elsewhere. However, the disclosure is not a qualifying disclosure if the person making it commits an offence by making it; nor will it be a qualifying disclosure if the information is subject to legal professional privilege, and had been disclosed to the person in the course of obtaining legal advice.

Protected Disclosure

A qualifying disclose will become a protected disclosure in the following circumstances:

(a) if the worker makes the disclosure to the employer, or to the person the worker reasonably believes is responsible for the relevant failure;

(b) if the disclosure is made in the course of obtaining legal advice;

(c) if the worker's employer is appointed by enactment by a Minister of the Crown, the disclosure is made in good faith to a Minister of the Crown;

(d) if the disclosure is made in good faith to a person prescribed by the Secretary of State for the purpose of the Act.

A disclosure made to a person other than the employer or a prescribed person may also qualify as a protected disclosure if, but only if, the worker making the disclosure:

(a) makes it in good faith;

(b) reasonably believes it to be true;

(c) does not make personal gain from the disclosure;

(d) reasonably believes that he would be subject to some detriment if he makes the disclosure to his employer;

(e) reasonably believes that relevant evidence would be concealed or destroyed if he makes the disclosure to his employer; and

(f) has already disclosed the same information to his employer or to a prescribed person.

In deciding whether it is reasonable for the worker to make the disclosure, regard will be had to, amongst other issues:

(a) the identity of the person to whom the disclosure is made;

(b) the seriousness of the relevant failure;

(c) whether the disclose relates to a past, present or future failure;

(d) whether the disclose breaches a duty of confidentiality owed by the employer to another person; and

(e) where the disclosure has already been made to the employer or a prescribed person, any action taken, or which should have been taken.

Exceptionally Serious Failures

In the case of an "exceptionally serious failure", regard need only be had to whether the worker makes the disclosure in good faith, believing it to be true; does not make personal gain from the disclosure, and in all the circumstances whether it was reasonable to make the disclosure; particularly in respect of the identity of the person to whom it was made.

FIXED-TERM EMPLOYEES (PREVENTION OF LESS FAVOURABLE TREATMENT) REGULATIONS 2002

From October 1, 2002, these Regulations, brought in under the Employment Act 2002, oblige all employers to treat fixed-term employees no less favourably than comparable permanent employees. Fixed-term employees are those working under a contract for a specific fixed time, for a specific task, or a contract which will terminate upon the happening, or non-happening, of some future event. The Regulations also limit the use of successive fixed-term contracts to a maximum of four years, unless objective justification for further periods can be shown by the employer; this is designed to prevent employers avoiding such employment rights as redundancy entitlements by the use of a series of fixed-term appointments. On this point it is worth considering the EAT decision in *Booth v USA* [1999] I.R.L.R. 16—an issue of continuity of employment.

Chapter Checklist

You should now know and understand:

- some of the legislation that impacts directly and indirectly on Employment Law.

QUESTION AND ANSWER

The Question

Discuss the impact and effects of the Human Rights Act 1998 on Employment Law.

Suggested points for consideration

The Convention appears initially to have little direct relevance to employment law.

The Human Rights Act is directly enforceable only against public bodies, but some institutions may amount to hybrids, and some public bodies may perform both public and private functions—there is still some confusion in these areas.

The legislation requires the courts to act compatibly with the Convention, see e.g. X v Y [2004] I.R.L.R. 625.

Issues concerning trade unions—freedom to join or not join, right to strike, etc.

Article 8—respect for private and family life etc. Issues of drug testing, monitoring of telephone calls, e-mails, employees' behaviour out of work.

"Direct" impact of ECtHR judgments.

Health and Safety

8

The aim of health and safety law is to prevent accidents occurring in the workplace. The enforcement of health and safety legislation differs from most other areas of employment law in that breach of a health and safety statute usually results in criminal liability. However, this does not prevent the injured party from pursuing a claim for damages in the event of an accident.

LEGISLATION HIGHLIGHTER

HEALTH AND SAFETY AT WORK ACT 1974

Sources of Health and Safety Law

The main sources of health and safety law in England and Wales are the common law, statute and European Legislation.

Much of the common law regarding health and safety as it relates to the individual employee is contained in the employer's implied term of duty of care. The major consolidating domestic legislation is the Health and Safety at Work Act 1974 (HSWA), which over the years has been supported and complimented by other legislation, including input from the EC.

The Treaty of Rome included art.118A, which states:

"The Member States shall pay particular attention to encouraging improvements, especially in the working environment, as regards the health and safety of workers, and shall set as their objective the harmonisation of conditions in this area, while maintaining the improvements."

One outcome of this has been the adoption of a Directive to encourage improvements in health and safety in the field of employment—the "Framework Directive"—Directive EC89/391.

. . . .

COMMON LAW

At common law the basis of the employer's duty towards his employees arises from the existence of the contract of employment. There is an implied term in the contract that the employer will take reasonable care to ensure the safety of his employees. Breach of this duty will amount to a breach of contract, and may allow the employee to leave, claim constructive dismissal and bring an action for unfair dismissal (see Unfair Dismissal).

In the case of injury to the employee, however, there is normally no advantage to suing in contract, and most claims are brought in the tort of negligence (*Donoghue v Stevenson* [1932] A.C. 562).

The employer's liability will arise in one of two ways. He will be directly responsible for his own actions or omissions which amount to negligence; he may also be responsible for the negligent actions or omissions of other employees, through the doctrine of vicarious liability.

Employer's Direct Liability
Under the common law, it is necessary to ask two questions:
(a) Was the injured party someone the employer should have reasonably foreseen would be likely to have been injured if the work had not been carried out properly?
(b) In all the circumstances did the employer attain the standard of care expected from a reasonable employer?

The Injured Party must Show Three Things:
(a) That the employer owed a duty of care.
(b) That there was a breach of that duty.
(c) That the breach was the cause of the injury.

Duty of Care
The duty of the employer is owed to the employee as an individual (*Paris v Stepney BC* [1951] A.C. 376), and consequently a higher standard of care may be owed to some employees than to others (*James v Hepworth & Grandage Ltd* [1968] 1 QB 94). The duty is owed by the employer, and may not be delegated—although the performance of the duty may be (*Wilsons and Clyde Coal Co Ltd v English* [1938] A.C. 57).

The duty is generally divided into four areas:
(a) Safe Plant and Equipment—reasonable steps should be taken by the employer to provide and maintain safe plant and equipment.
(b) Safe Place of Work—the employer has a duty to take reasonable steps to ensure that the workplace is safe, not only for his employees, but also for anyone else who may use the premises (Occupiers Liability Act 1957 and 1984).

BRADFORD V ROBINSON RENTALS [1967] 1 ALL E.R. 267
In a particularly cold spell an employee was instructed to make a delivery involving a round trip of some 400 miles, in a van which had no heating and badly fitting windows. He suffered frostbite and brought an action against his employer.

Held: The employer was liable for failing to provide suitable and safe plant and equipment.

LATIMER V AEC LTD [1953] A.C. 643
Rain had flooded a factory floor, which had become slippery with a mixture of oil and water. Sawdust was laid over most of the floor, but there was not sufficient sawdust to cover the entire floor. An employee slipped on part of the untreated floor and was injured.

Held: The employer was held not liable. Reasonable precautions had been taken, and the court held that the danger was not sufficient to warrant closing the factory entirely.

(c) Safe System of Work—the employer has a duty to ensure that the methods used to undertake the work are safe. This includes the system, training, supervision, protective clothing, warnings, etc.

The employer is responsible for ensuring that the system is carried out, and must bear in mind that employees may be forgetful or lazy, however the employer may not be liable in cases of disobedience.

MCWILLIAMS V SIR WILLIAM ARROL & CO LTD [1962] 1 ALL E.R. 623
Steel erectors working on a building site were provided with safety belts, which they chose not to wear. The belts were removed to another site, and shortly afterwards one of the employees on the first site fell and was killed.

Held: The employer was not held liable for the death, as it was shown that the employees had always chosen not to wear them (see also the issue of Causation).

(d) Provision of Competent Fellow Employees—the employer has a duty to recruit and train competent fellow employees, this may include the dismissal of incompetent workers.

KEY CASE

HUDSON V RIDGE MANUFACTURING CO LTD [1957] 2 QB 348
For a number of years an employee had played practical jokes including tripping fellow employees. On one occasion an employee sustained a serious injury, and brought an action against the employer.

Held: The employer was aware of the horseplay over a number of years but had taken no action to stop it; thus they were held liable.

Breach of Duty
The claimant must show that the employer's actions fell below the standard expected of a reasonable employer.

Obviously, the greater the risk, the greater the care required; and the more likely the risk, the more necessary the care. In deciding how a reasonable employer would have acted in a given situation, the court will take into account the cost of the action necessary (see *Latimer v AEC Ltd* where the only alternative to the employer would have been to close the factory entirely).

Breach as the Cause of the Injury
The breach must be the cause of the injury. See, for example, *McWilliams v Sir William Arrol & Co Ltd*, where even though the employer was in breach of his duty by removing the safety belts, evidence showed that even if they had been present the employees would not have used them. Thus the employer's breach was held not to be the cause of the injury.

The normal tort rules of remoteness apply, thus if the employer is negligent in respect of a foreseeable type of injury he will be liable for all loss of that type arising from his action.

Defences
There are two main defences available:
(a) Contributory negligence on the part of the employee, in which case the court has discretion under the **Law Reform (Contributory Negligence) Act 1945** to reduce proportionally the damages payable.
(b) Consent to the risk by the employee (*volenti non fit injuria*). This is a complete defence, but the courts are aware that in reality employees very rarely give real consent to injury.

ICI Ltd v Shatwell [1965] A.C. 656
Two shotfirers deliberately broke both statutory regulations and the employer's instructions, resulting in injury to both of them. One of them then brought an action against the employer on the basis of their vicarious liability for the actions of the other shotfirer.

Held: The employer was not liable, the complete defence of *volenti non fit injuria* succeeded.

Occupational Stress

The issue of employer's liability for occupational stress and work-related psychiatric injury is a complex one. In the case of *Walker v Northumberland CC* [1995] I.R.L.R. 35 the court held that the employer was liable in respect of a second nervous breakdown suffered by its employee. Mr Walker had suffered a first nervous breakdown due to increased workload and staff shortages. He returned to work, having been promised and received, additional staff. However, the additional staff were subsequently withdrawn and Mr Walker suffered a second nervous breakdown. The court held that there had been adequate warning signs to which the employer should have reacted.

In 2002 the Court of Appeal heard the joined cases of *Sutherland v Hatton*; *Somerset CC v Barber*; *Sandwell MBC v Jones*; *Baker Refractories v Bishop* [2002] I.R.L.R. 263, and laid down a 16 point guideline for dealing with similar cases; these guidelines were impliedly approved by the House of Lords in *Barber v Somerset CC* [2004] I.R.L.R. 475.

Application of the guidelines may be seen in the Court of Appeal decisions in the joined cases of *Hartman v South Essex Mental Health and Community Care NHS Trust*; *Best v Staffordshire University*; *Green v Grimsby & Scunthorpe Newspapers Ltd*; *Melville v Home Office*; *Wheeldon v HSBC Bank Ltd* [2005] I.R.L.R. 293. It should be stressed that, in view of the complexity of the issues and issues of public policy raised, each case must be viewed on its own facts (e.g. *Intel Corp. v Daw* [2007] IRLR 355 cf. *Dickens v O2 plc* [2009] IRLR 58)

Employer's Indirect Liability

If a third party is injured due to the negligence of an employee, the employer may be liable under the doctrine of vicarious liability, but only if the employee is acting in the course of his employment.

The concept of "in the course of employment" as used in tort is no longer the same as is used in cases of discrimination (see chapter

"Discrimination"). In discrimination cases the courts now interpret the phrase in the way that a layman would understand it, following the Court of Appeal decision in *Jones v Tower Boot Co Ltd*. In tort cases, however, the phrase is still interpreted more strictly, and is taken generally to mean that the employer will only be vicariously liable for the actions of his employees if the actions are carried out with the authority of the employer; although it is necessary to bear in mind the House of Lords ruling in *Lister v Hesley Hall Ltd* [2001] I.R.L.R. 472, which in at least some scenarios (the case concerns issues of sexual abuse by an employee towards children in the employer's care) redefines and broadens the common law test.

KEY CASE

KAY V ITW LTD [1968] 1 QB 140
A fork lift truck driver found that his way was blocked by a lorry. Although he had no specific instruction to do so, he moved the lorry himself, and in so doing injured another employee.

Held: The employer was held to be vicariously liable, since the action was not so extreme as to take it outside of his normal activities.

KEY CASE

HILTON V THOMAS BURTON LTD [1961] 1 W.L.R. 705
An employee made use of a firm's van to drive to a cafe on an unauthorised work break. In so doing he knocked down and killed a fellow worker.

Held: Although the employee had the general permission of the employer to drive the van, at the time of the incident he was acting outside the course of his employment. Thus the employer was not liable.

The Tort of Breach of Statutory Duty

There is no automatic presumption that all breaches of statutory duties are actionable in the civil court (*Cutler v Wandsworth Stadium Ltd* [1949] A.C. 398). Many recent statutes make clear that a breach will give rise to an action for breach of statutory duty, e.g. s.47(2) of the Health and Safety at Work Act 1974 (discussed below), but the issue is far less clear with older legislation.

There are four elements to the tort. The claimant must show, first, that he is within the class of person the legislation was designed to protect; second, that the injury sustained is of a type that the legislation was intended to prevent; third, that the company, the defendant, is actually in breach of the duty; and finally, the question of causation must be satisfied.

STATUTE

The main and most important piece of domestic legislation is the Health and Safety at Work Act 1974 (HSWA). It is a complex and detailed piece of legislation, which when introduced had far reaching consequences for health and safety in the workplace.

The Act imposes a duty on employees to act reasonably. Sections 7 and 8 state that the employee should take reasonable care, both for his own safety and for the safety of others. The employee is also under a duty to cooperate with the employer in carrying out the Health and Safety policy, which each employer must prepare under s.2(3).

The main thrust of the Act, however, is aimed at the employer. Section 2 states that it is the duty of every employer to ensure, so far as is reasonably practicable, the health, safety and welfare at work of all his employees, including the maintenance of safe systems of work, safe place of work, safe working environment and adequate training.

"So far as is reasonably practicable" does not mean that the employer has an absolute duty to eliminate all risks.

KEY CASE

WEST BROMWICH BUILDING SOCIETY V TOWNSEND [1983] I.C.R. 257
An HSE inspector alleged that the employer had not taken reasonable steps to ensure the protection of its staff by failing to erect bandit screens on its counters.

Held: Since the danger of attack was relatively slight, the staff had all been trained not to resist attack, and the screens would appear contrary to the society's customer friendly image, the court held that the society had done everything reasonably practicable.

Additionally, the Act provides for:
(a) The establishment of the Health and Safety Commission, an advisory body appointed by the Secretary of State to secure the health, safety and welfare of workers. It also proposes new legislation and standards.

(b) The establishment of a unified enforcement procedure under the HSE, which has a staff of over 4500, including inspectors, policy advisors, technical and medical experts. The HSE also publishes a number of Approved Codes of Practice and Guidance Notes.

If an HSE inspector is of the opinion that an employer is contravening the Act, ss.21 and 22 gives him the power to issue an improvement notice requiring that the problem be remedied, or in the case of serious danger, a prohibition notice requiring that an activity be discontinued until the situation is remedied.

Furthermore, the Act is an enabling Act, and has been used to implement EC Directives.

EC Framework Directive

EC Directive 89/391 concerning the harmonisation of health and safety legislation in Europe, along with six other directives concerning specific subjects were implemented by a series of regulations introduced at the beginning of 1993.

(a) Management of Health and Safety at Work Regulations 1992. The framework regulations, imposing a duty on employers to carry out risk assessment measures, put into practice preventative measures, and nominate health and safety representatives.

(b) Provision and Use of Work Equipment Regulations 1992.

(c) Manual Handling Operations Regulations 1992.

(d) Workplace (Health, Safety and Welfare) Regulations 1992. This replaces much existing legislation concerning work environment, provision of workplace facilities, etc.

(e) Personal Protective Equipment at Work Regulations 1992.

(f) Health and Safety (Display Screen Equipment) Regulations 1992.

KEY CASE

STARK V THE POST OFFICE [2000] I.C.R. 1013

Mr Stark worked for the Post Office as a postman delivering letters, for which purpose the Post Office provided him with a bicycle. One day the front brake on the bicycle broke, causing the wheel to jam and Mr Stark to be thrown to the floor, where he sustained injuries.

Both parties accepted that a prior examination of the bicycle would not have revealed the defect, and consequently there was no way in which the employer could have had prior warning of the accident. However, it was argued for Mr Stark that reg.6 of the Provision and Use of Work Equipment Regulations 1992 imposed an absolute obligation on the employer to ensure that the equipment was maintained in good repair.

Held: Although the Directives (Work Equipment Directive 89/655 and Framework Directive 89/391) may be read as laying down a less than absolute duty, the same could not be said of the Regulations, which had been drafted so as to impose an absolute duty on the employer.

Commentary
The Regulations thus impose an absolute, strict liability on the employer, which is, of course, a far higher level of duty than is imposed by common law.

Chapter Checklist

You should now know and understand:

- **the scope of the employer's duty;**
- **differences in the level of duty of care owed;**
- **issues regarding occupational stress and psychiatric injury.**

QUESTION AND ANSWER

The Question

"The recent increase in claims against employers for work related stress and psychiatric injury has required the courts to lay down guidelines which are already being tested and perhaps found wanting."

Discuss.

Suggested points for consideration

The employer's general duty of care.

The case of *Walker v Northumberland CC*.

Discussion of the Court of Appeal's guidelines in *Sutherland v Hatton et al.*

The application of those guidelines in cases such as *Hartman v S Essex et al.*

Possible relaxation of standards in such as *Dickens v O2.*

Termination of Employment

9

There are three main methods by which employment may be terminated: termination by way of contract, termination in breach of contract, and termination by methods external to the contract.

Termination by Way of Contract

Every contract of employment should contain, as a term of the contract, details of how the contract may be lawfully determined by either party. Except in certain circumstances, this will involve one party giving notice to the other party. Such notice period should be no less than the statutory minimum laid down in s.86 of the ERA 1996.

Under s.86 minimum notice periods are as follows:

(a) employed for between one month and two years—one weeks' notice
(b) employed for between two and 12 years—one week for each year of employment; or
(c) employed for over 12 years—12 weeks' notice.

These will apply where either no notice period is quoted in the contract, or the notice period stated in the contract is less than this. If the contractual notice period is longer, the longer period will apply.

It is, of course, possible for the employee to determine the contract for any reason by giving the required amount of notice. Failure to give such notice would allow the employer to bring an action for breach of contract, but in practice and for a number of reasons this is rarely done.

Statute has imposed certain restrictions and obligations on the part of the employer when seeking to determine the employment contract and so dismiss the employee. Not only does the employee have the right to certain minimum notice periods (s.86 of the ERA 1996), there is also a right not to be unfairly dismissed (s.94 of the ERA 1996), and a right to compensation if the reason for dismissal is redundancy (s.135 of the ERA 1996).

Termination in Breach of Contract

If the contract of employment is terminated by the employer—in other words if the employee is dismissed—in circumstances or for reasons outside of the contractual terms, the dismissal will constitute a breach of contract by the employer. This will allow the employee in many cases to bring an action for either wrongful dismissal or unfair dismissal.

In theory, if the employee was to terminate the contract in circumstances or for reasons outside of the contractual terms, this would allow the employer to bring an action for breach of contract. However, in practice this very rarely happens. Most companies would not wish to sue an ex-employee for damages in such circumstances, partly because the chances of financial success are in reality small, and partly because such action would probably give rise to adverse publicity.

A further factor is that s.236 of the Trade Union and Labour Relations (Consolidation) Act 1992 states:

"No court shall, whether by way of—

(a) an order for specific performance or specific implement of a contract of employment, or

(b) an injunction or interdict restraining a breach or threatened breach of such a contract.

compel an employee to do any work or attend at any place for the doing of any work."

Thus the courts may not enforce a contract of employment against an employee so as to force the employee either to work or to attend for work. (For a narrow but apparently just interpretation of this law, see the case of *Evening Standard v Henderson* [1987] I.C.R. 588.)

Termination by Methods External to the Contract

Since in many respects the employment contract is similar to any other contract, the doctrine of frustration of contract applies to it.

Frustration may be defined as an act external to the contract which is not caused by the fault of either party, and which was not foreseen by the parties to the contract (and thus not planned for within the contract), which has the effect of fundamentally altering the contract, or making it impossible to perform.

The effect of frustration on the contract of employment is that the contract is held to be immediately terminated without a dismissal taking place. Since, in law, no dismissal has taken place, the ex-employee will be unable to claim either wrongful dismissal or unfair dismissal.

In order to decide whether the employment contract has been frustrated, and to an extent to mitigate the harshness to the employee in such situations, a number of factors for consideration were laid down in the case of *Egg Stores (Stamford Hill) Ltd v Leibovici* [1977] I.C.R. 260, including length of previous employment, nature of the job, nature and effect of the disabling event, the requirement for a replacement, whether a reasonable employer could be expected to wait any longer, etc.

Examples of frustration of the contract of employment include:

(a) Imposition of a prison sentence (*FC Shepherd & Co Ltd v Jerrom* [1986] I.R.L.R. 358). It has been argued that the imposition of a prison sentence must amount to the fault of the employee, thus it cannot constitute frustration. Although there is some logic in this, if it were accepted, it would mean that an employee sentenced to imprisonment would be able to sue for wrongful dismissal if given no notice period, or even for unfair dismissal; whilst an employee whose contract was frustrated through illness would have no such recourse. This would give a situation in which the employee at fault is in a better position than the employee whose contract is terminated through no fault of their own. The court in *Shepherd v Jerrom* considered such a situation to be "an affront to common sense", and therefore held that imprisonment could lead to frustration—holding that it was not the commission of the offence which was the frustrating event, but the imposition of the prison sentence.

(b) Medical evidence that the worker could probably never work again (*Notcutt v Universal Equipment Co Ltd* [1986] I.R.L.R. 218). In cases of long term sickness, the court will consider such factors as how long the employee is expected to be absent, the need of the employer to obtain a replacement, how long the employee has been employed, the provision of sick pay within the contract, etc. Long term absence from work will not automatically constitute frustration.

The courts are unwilling to find frustration of employment contracts too readily; in *Williams v Watson Luxury Coaches Ltd* [1990] I.R.L.R. 164 it was stated that frustration in employment would be a rare occurrence, and the doctrine should be severely limited.

Death of the Employer

At common law the death of the employer would have the effect of terminating the contract of employment without giving rise to a dismissal. In similar circumstances, however, statute would deem a dismissal to have taken place (s.136(5) of the ERA 1996).

Chapter Checklist

You should now know and understand:

- **the three different methods by which a contract of employment may be terminated.**

QUESTION AND ANSWER

The Question

Advise XCo in the following situations:

a) The company wishes to dismiss John, one of their warehouse operatives, who has just been sentenced to six months imprisonment.

b) The company is concerned that Keith and Larry, delivery drivers, are working during their holidays for one of XCo's competitors, and may pass on trade secrets.

Suggested points for consideration

a) Regarding John, the company would appear to have two options. Firstly, they may dismiss him on the grounds either of "conduct" or "some other substantial reason". The tribunal may take into account such factors as whether John's conduct occurred inside or outside of his employment, whether his conduct has a bearing on his ability to do his job, etc., but there is plenty of case law to suggest that the dismissal would be held to be fair (e.g. *Mathewson v RB Wilson Dental Laboratories*)—particularly if the company acts within the ACAS code of practice.

The company's second option would be to declare that John's term of imprisonment has frustrated the contract (*Shepherd v Jerrom*), and thus the contract is automatically terminated without a dismissal taking place. Again, the tribunal would consider such factors as length of sentence, need for the employee's work to be done, availability of a replacement, etc.

b) Regarding Keith and Larry, the court must balance a reluctance to restrict the ability of individuals to increase their earnings through spare time working, with the right of a company to protect its legitimate interests (*Hivac v Park Royal Scientific*). The company may either attempt to obtain an injunction to prevent its employees being employed elsewhere during the existence of their contract of employment, or it may wish to dismiss the employees, claiming that they are in breach of faith. However, be aware of such case law as *Nova Plastics v Froggatt*, in which the dismissal of an odd-job man for part time working with a competitor was held to be unfair, in view of the fact that due to his position he was hardly likely to cause any harm to his employers.

Wrongful Dismissal

10

THE BASIC POSITION

An action for wrongful dismissal is a common law action for damages to compensate the ex-employee for losses suffered for the wrongful termination of the employment contract. Generally this will only amount to monies to which the employee would have been contractually entitled had the contract been lawfully terminated, in effect, monies in lieu of notice.

Normally such damages will be limited to either wages for the minimum statutory notice period, or the notice period stipulated by the contract, whichever is the longer. The damages represent only the basic wages and other contractual entitlements; there is no entitlement to any discretionary payments, e.g. bonus or salary increases, etc. Thus, an action for wrongful dismissal concerns only whether the correct contractual notice period has been given, as such, the reason for the dismissal is irrelevant (*Addis v Gramophone Co Ltd* [1909] A.C. 488). Remember, of course, that in a number of circumstances an employer may summarily dismiss an employee quite lawfully, e.g. for gross misconduct (see *Sinclair v Neighbour* [1967] 2 QB 279, *Pepper v Webb* [1969] 1 W.L.R. 514 cf. *Wilson v Racher* [1974] I.C.R. 428).

Other Developments

In most circumstances, the employer will be able to discharge their obligations under the contract by paying money in lieu of notice, and not requiring or not allowing the employee to work a notice period. There are, however, some situations where such action may in itself constitute a separate breach of contract, e.g. actors or others whose work requires them to be exposed or displayed to the public. In such cases the courts have been prepared to award separate damages for damage to reputation (*Herbert Clayton & Jack Waller Ltd v Oliver* [1930] A.C. 209).

In the case of *Malik v BCCI SA* [1997] I.R.L.R. 462 the House of Lords held that where the manner of the dismissal constituted a breach of the contractual term of mutual trust and confidence and this caused financial loss, that loss may be recoverable in an action for wrongful dismissal (cf. *Addis* above). Although the House of Lords implied that this apparent extension to *Addis* was confined to the facts of the *BCCI* case, it may well prove useful precedent in future cases; although on a slightly different issue the House of Lords in *Johnson v Unisys Ltd* [2001] I.R.L.R. 279 refused to extend the remedies available in the common law where statute already provided a remedy by way of compensation for unfair dismissal. The *Johnson* approach was followed in *Eastwood v Magnox Electric Plc* [2004] I.R.L.R. 733, HL, and in *Dunnachie v Kingston upon Hull CC* [2004] I.R.L.R. 727 the House of Lords confirmed that it was not possible to recover non-economic loss, such as for injury to feelings.

The Effect of the Repudiatory Breach

It is sometimes necessary to decide whether the terms of the employment contract can exist once the repudiatory breach—the wrongful dismissal—has taken place; in other words, does the breach itself bring the contract to an end (the automatic or unilateral theory), or is it necessary for the innocent party, the employee, to accept the breach to make it effective and end the contractual relationship (the elective or bilateral theory).

Common sense might suggest that the employment relationship is at an end and thus the contract is terminated once the dismissal has taken place; but the general law of contract makes it clear that the breach will only become effective on the contract once it has been accepted by the innocent party. Much of the case law relevant to this issue has concerned instances where the employee has sought to restrain the employer from terminating the contract until a contractually agreed disciplinary procedure has taken place, consequently it is perhaps not surprising that the courts have inclined towards the elective or bilateral theory in order to keep the contract alive whilst correct procedures are followed by both parties (*Gunton v Richmond upon Thames LBC* [1980] I.C.R. 755, *Thomas Marshall (Exports) Ltd v Guinle* [1979] ch.227, etc).

However, it must surely also be true that the employment relationship is of a purely personal nature, and as such the contract cannot continue to exist once the relationship has been effectively terminated by a repudiatory breach.

Authority to support this automatic or unilateral theory may be found in *Sanders v Ernest A Neale Ltd* [1974] I.R.L.R. 236 and as obiter dicta in *Boyo v Lambeth LBC* [1995] I.R.L.R. 50.

A method of viewing this problem, which has the effect of reconciling at least some of the otherwise conflicting case law, is to consider that, in contract law, an innocent party may only refuse to accept a repudiatory contract breach if they have a "legitimate interest" in maintaining the contract. Thus, maintaining the contract during disciplinary procedure may well be a "legitimate interest"; wishing to continue to draw wages whilst not having to work, may not be.

The court in *Irani v Southampton and South West Hampshire Health Authority* [1985] I.C.R. 590 chose not to address this issue, but granted an injunction preventing a dismissal in order to allow time for a disciplinary procedure to take place, in circumstances where it was held that mutual trust and confidence between the parties still existed.

KEY CASE

ADDIS V GRAMOPHONE CO LTD [1909] A.C. 488

Mr Addis's contract provided that he would be paid part salary and part commission, and in the event of termination would be entitled to six months' notice. His contract was terminated by his employers and he was given six months' notice, but was not allowed to work out his notice period. The question arose as to the damages to which Mr Addis was entitled.

Held: The House of Lords held that he was entitled only to the wages for the six month notice period, plus the commission he would have earned had he been permitted to work for those six months.

He was not entitled to damages as compensation for injured feelings, nor for "the loss he may sustain from the fact that his having been dismissed of itself makes it more difficult for him to obtain fresh employment." per Lord Loreburn L.C.

Commentary

Thus compensation for wrongful dismissal amounts only to monies to which the employee would have been entitled under the contract. It will not include any discretionary bonuses or pay rises.

KEY CASE

MALIK V BCCI SA [1997] I.R.L.R. 462

Mr Malik was dismissed through redundancy, following the collapse of the bank through "dishonest and corrupt business" practices. Mr Malik claimed damages for the disadvantage his association with the bank would place him under in trying to obtain further employment. It was argued that following Addis such damages were not available.

Held: The House of Lords held that Addis did not preclude the award of damages in a situation such as this, since the damages in *Malik* were in respect of the employer's breach of the contract term of mutual trust and confidence. At the time of Addis this contract term had not been recognised, whereas today it is implied into every employment contract; accordingly damages should be assessed for the breach of the term in line with accepted contract principles.

Commentary

On the particular facts of this case, the decision would appear to be both sensible and fair, and reflect current business realities. Although the court suggested that the decision would have little effect beyond the specifics of this case, it is very likely that future claimants would wish to rely on it.

KEY CASE

JOHNSON v UNISYS LTD [2001] I.R.L.R. 279

Mr Johnson had worked for Unisys from 1971 until 1987, when he was made redundant. From 1985 he had suffered from work related stress requiring him to take time off from work. In 1990 he was re-employed by Unisys, until 1994 when he was dismissed on the grounds of misconduct. He made a successful complaint of unfair dismissal for which the tribunal awarded him compensation.

Mr Johnson then made a further complaint for wrongful dismissal claiming that the manner of his dismissal had caused psychiatric injury and a loss of some £400,000 in earnings.

Held: The House of Lords upheld the dismissal of his claim. In somewhat conflicting opinions (two of their Lordships were prepared to depart from the accepted ratio of *Addis*), the majority upheld *Addis*, and distinguished *BCCI* on its facts. It was held that, since parliament had intended that claims concerning manner of dismissal were dealt with as statutory unfair dismissal claims and had placed a financial ceiling on such claims, it was not for the court to undermine the intention of parliament.

Commentary

It is therefore necessary (although sometimes by no means easy) to distinguish between

(a) a breach of contract which forms part of the dismissal and for which the remedy is a statutory claim for unfair dismissal; and

(b) a breach which does not form part of the dismissal and for which the remedy may be a common law claim for breach of contract.

It will generally be financially beneficial for an applicant to claim under unfair dismissal legislation, but in the case of Mr Johnson and some others this will not be so—Mr Johnson sought some £400,000 damages but was able to claim only the statutory maximum for unfair dismissal which was (at that time) £11,000.

Public Law Remedies

Certain public employees may be entitled to public law remedies against their employer, by way of judicial review. This may result in a quashing order (previously known as an order for "certiorari"), quashing the decision of the employer, or a mandatory order (previously known as "mandamus"), an order requiring an employer to perform a duty.

The circumstances in which public employees may rely on public law are very limited. In *R. v East Berkshire Area Health Authority, Ex p. Walsh* [1984] I.C.R. 743 the Court of Appeal held that judicial review would only be available where either the matter concerned public rather than private law or where the employment relationship is not defined in contractual terms (see *Ridge v Baldwin* [1964] A.C. 40), thus most public employees would need to rely on private law for an action regarding breach of the employment contract.

Chapter Checklist

You should now know and understand:

- **the scope of the common law action for wrongful dismissal;**

- **the limitations on damages awardable;**

- **the importance of the term of mutual trust and confidence in a claim for wrongful dismissal;**

- **the limitation on claims for a breach of contractual term if that breach forms part of the dismissal;**

- **the limited availability of public law remedies.**

QUESTION AND ANSWER

Gertrude has been employed as an invoice clerk by XCo Ltd for the past five years. In previous years all the staff in her department have received annual pay increases including Gertrude, but this year she discovers that she is the only person not to receive a rise.

When Gertrude sees the personnel manager to ask why, she is told: "Your work is not up to standard. Why don't you just take the hint and resign?"

Gertrude is very upset, she says the comment is very unfair and she cannot accept it. Gertrude continues to work at XCo until last week, when she announced her immediate resignation and walked out.

Advise XCo Ltd of their legal position in relation to her departure from the company.

Suggested points for consideration

The question concerns the issue of constructive dismissal. Have either the actions of the company in failing to award Gertrude a pay rise, or the words of the personnel manager, amounted to a repudiation by the company of the contract, which would allow Gertrude to leave and claim constructive dismissal?

Unless an employee has a term in the employment contract to the contrary, there is no implied term that pay increases will be awarded (*Murco Petroleum v Forge*); although if an employer acts capriciously in withholding a pay increase that may amount to a breach of the implied term of mutual trust and confidence (*United Bank v Akhtar*, and obiter in *Murco*).

The words used by the personnel manager may constitute a breach of the term of mutual trust and confidence. That would be a question of fact for the tribunal, who would consider such factors as the relationship between the parties, any prior history, etc. (*Isle of Wight Tourist Board v Coombes*).

By continuing to work Gertrude may have affirmed the contract, much would depend upon how much time elapsed between the incident and her leaving, and also upon whether she had made it clear

WRONGFUL DISMISSAL

that she did not accept the situation (*Marriott v Oxford Co-op*), although there is a difference between accepting a situation, and not objecting to a situation (*Harlow v Artemis Intl. Corp.*)

Unfair Dismissal

11

LEGISLATION HIGHLIGHTER

EMPLOYMENT RIGHTS ACT 1996 SECTIONS 94–98

Unfair Dismissal is a statutory concept consolidated almost wholly within the ERA 1996. Section 94(1) of the ERA 1996 states: "An employee has the right not to be unfairly dismissed by his employer."

Different writers and commentators have used various formats in order to explain and try to simplify the issue of unfair dismissal. Unfair Dismissal is a very broad topic and one which is almost guaranteed to appear in any employment law examination in one guise or another. It overlaps into several other areas, and can appear a daunting subject to many students. However, approached properly, it is one of the most straightforward topics in employment law.

An examination question on Unfair Dismissal may be successfully attempted by logically working through the following four steps in order—this will both give a structure to the answer and ensure that all aspects of the question are considered:

(a) Can the applicant claim?
(b) Can a dismissal be identified?
(c) The reason for the dismissal.
(d) The fairness of the dismissal.

It is of course necessary to consider each question in detail:

CAN THE APPLICANT CLAIM?

(a) Is the applicant an employee?
It is necessary that the applicant proves their employee status as considered in ch.3 in order to qualify for unfair dismissal rights. However, be aware that under the Employment Relations Act 1999 powers have been granted to the relevant Minister to extend existing employment rights to categories of workers not presently covered.

(b) Does the employee belong to an excluded group?

Certain categories of employees automatically fall outside the protection of the Act, these include:

(i) share fishermen

(ii) the police, and in certain circumstances crown servants;

(iii) those protected by collective agreements regulating dismissal procedures may be exempted—such procedures must be approved by the Secretary for State as operating as a substitute for the statutory scheme (s.110 of the ERA 1996). At present no such schemes are in operation.

(c) Does the employee have the minimum required length of continuous service?

Following The Unfair Dismissal and Statement of Reasons for Dismissal (Variation of Qualifying Period) Order 1999, SI 1999/1436, the minimum period of continuous employment required in order to claim for unfair dismissal is one year (at the time of writing, it has been suggested that the one year qualifying period be extended). In some circumstances it will be necessary to consider what is meant by the term "continuous employment".

Continuity of Employment may be considered under two sub-headings: continuity within the contract of employment, and continuity outside the contract.

Continuity within the Contract

Weeks which count towards continuity are "any week during the whole or part of which the employee's relations with the employer are governed by a contract of employment" (s.212(1) of the ERA 1996). Thus continuity may be maintained should the terms of the contract change, the place of work or job function change, and even across a series of consecutive contracts with the same employer. Any term of the contract purporting to waive continuity rights would be void under s.203 of the ERA 1996.

Continuity Outside the Contract

Statute protects continuity in certain circumstances where no contract of employment is in force; these are for up to 26 weeks of sickness or injury, due to a temporary cessation of work, or in circumstances whereby through custom or arrangement such absences are not regarded as breaking continuity (s.212(3) of the ERA 1996).

Examples of such situations include:

(i) Continuity was preserved for a lecturer working under a series of contracts each year from September to July, even though for the months between there was no contract subsisting. The House of Lords held that the summer months constituted a "temporary cessation of work" (*Ford v Warwickshire CC* [1983] I.R.L.R. 126).

(ii) Workers laid off and taken back on again, possibly on a number of occasions over several years, due to seasonal demand may also have continuity of employment (*Flack v Kodak Ltd* [1986] I.C.R. 775).

(iii) In deciding whether gaps in employment are sufficient to break continuity, the court in Ford adopted a mathematical approach by comparing the period of the break with the periods of work on either side of it, to determine whether it was "temporary". The court in Flack, however, used a broad brush approach to determine overall whether continuity had been preserved, rather than to examine each instance of cessation of work in its own right. Although these two methods of approach appear to be in conflict, the EAT in the case of *Sillars v Charrington Fuels Ltd* [1988] I.C.R. 505 suggested that the mathematical approach should be used when gaps are regular, but the broad brush approach was appropriate where gaps were irregular.

(iv) The EAT has cast some doubt on the issue of preserving continuity of employment with the decision in *Booth v United States of America* [1999] I.R.L.R. 16, in which it was stated:

"whilst it is generally desirable that employees should enjoy statutory protection during their employment, Parliament has laid down the conditions under which that protection is afforded. If, by so arranging their affairs, an employer is lawfully able to employ people in such a manner that the employees cannot complain of unfair dismissal or seek a redundancy payment, that is a matter for him. The courts simply try and apply the law as it stands."

This decision may weaken the line of authority from Flack, Ford and Sillars etc.

(v) Weeks lost through industrial action will neither count towards nor break continuity of employment (s.216 of the ERA 1996).

In some situations another factor which may affect the qualifying period of service is the question of the effective date of termination of the contract.

The effective date of termination (EDT) is defined in s.97 of the ERA 1996 as:

"where notice is given, the date on which that notice expires, b) where no notice is given, the date on which the termination takes place, or c) in the event of a fixed term contract not being renewed, the date on which the contract expires."

Some confusion has arisen in determining the EDT in cases of termination with money in lieu of notice. The traditional approach in *Dedman v British Building and Engineering Appliances Ltd* [1974] I.C.R. 53 was to treat money in lieu of notice as a summary dismissal and hold that the EDT was on the date the termination takes place, i.e. the final day of employment. However the case of *Adams v GKN Sankey Ltd* [1980] I.R.L.R. 416 suggested that the EDT should depend upon the true construction placed on the dismissal; if the dismissal was expressed as summary dismissal, but with monies in respect of possible damages for wrongful dismissal, then the EDT should be the date of termination; if, on the other hand, the dismissal was with notice, but monies representing wages in lieu of notice were given, then the EDT should be the date on which the notice would expire. Although there is no binding authority on the point, *Adams* is to be preferred.

In cases where the contract is terminated by the employer and the minimum notice periods provided for by s.86 of the ERA 1996 would, if given, expire on a later date than the EDT, statute (s.97(2) of the of the ERA 1996) will intervene to hold that the later date is the EDT for the purpose of calculating the qualifying period of employment under s.108.

(d) Has the claim been brought within time?

Section 111 of the ERA states that claims of unfair dismissal must be brought before the tribunal within three months of the EDT, although s.111(2)(b) allows such further time as the tribunal considers reasonable if it considers that it was not reasonably practicable for the applicant to bring the case earlier. The courts have tended to interpret s.111(2)(b) strictly.

(i) Ignorance of one's rights will not normally be sufficient (*Dedman v British Building and Engineering Appliances* [1974] I.C.R. 53).

(ii) Incorrect advice from a skilled advisor may not be sufficient (*Riley v Tesco Stores Ltd* [1980] I.C.R. 323).

(iii) Waiting for the outcome of a relevant event, e.g. a criminal trial, may not be sufficient (*Norgett v Luton Industrial Co-op Soc Ltd* [1976] I.C.R. 442)

(iv) Waiting for the outcome of an internal appeal system undertaken following termination may not be sufficient (*Palmer v Southend-on-Sea BC* [1984] I.C.R. 372). In such circumstances the applicant should either enter an application to the tribunal immediately following termination, or should advise the tribunal office that an investigation is being undertaken.

(v) However, in the case of *Marks & Spencer Plc v Williams Ryan* [2005] I.R.L.R. 562 the court took a more relaxed view of an applicant who on the advice of the Citizen's Advice Bureau awaited the outcome of an internal appeal and by so doing submitted her claim to the tribunal after the three month period had expired. The claim was allowed to proceed.

(vi) In *Fishley v Working Men's College* (2004) EAT an application faxed to the tribunal offices 11 minutes after the three month time limit had expired was rejected.

CAN A DISMISSAL BE IDENTIFIED?

In many situations there will be no problem in identifying the dismissal, e.g. "You are fired", "I'm afraid I must give you a month's notice", etc. However, in some cases the situation is much less clear.

Words and Actions

(a) If the words are clear and unambiguous the tribunal should treat them as such (*Sothern v Franks Charlesly & Co* 1981] I.R.L.R. 278).

(b) If the words are ambiguous, if they have been said in the heat of the moment, or as part of an argument or row, the tribunal may look behind the actual words used to ensure that what has taken place really is a dismissal (*Chesham Shipping Ltd v Rowe* [1977] I.R.L.R. 391).

(c) Language which may constitute a dismissal in one industry or situation, may not have the same meaning in another (*Futty v D and D Brekkes Ltd* [1974] I.R.L.R. 130).

(d) It may often be possible for words said in the heat of the moment to be withdrawn (*Martin v Yeoman Aggregates Ltd* [1983] I.R.L.R. 49), but in some cases the mere saying of the words may destroy the contractual term of mutual trust and confidence.

(e) An employee prompted to resign by the threat of dismissal, may be held to have been dismissed (*East Sussex CC v Walker* (1972) 7 I.T.R. 280).

(f) However, if the resignation is prompted not by threat of dismissal, but by the offer of a severance package, there will not be a dismissal (*Birch v University of Liverpool* [1985] I.C.R. 470).

Resignation whilst under Notice of Dismissal

If an employee is under notice of dismissal, but then gives notice of resignation to take effect before the dismissal, statute provides that for the purposes of any unfair dismissal claim the employee shall be taken to have been dismissed (s.95(2) of the ERA 1996).

Dismissal whilst Continuing in Employment

Under normal circumstances, once a dismissal takes place the employment relationship will end. However, this is not always the case. In the case of *Hogg v Dover College* [1990] I.C.R. 39, Mr Hogg, a full-time teacher, suffered an illness and was subsequently offered part time work at a reduced salary. He worked part time under protest but also lodged a complaint of unfair dismissal. The EAT held that he had been dismissed from his full time position and that his part time work was being performed under a new contract.

It is unclear how widely this approach may be used by employees to fight unilaterally imposed changes to the contract of employment; by arguing that the change imposed by the employer has caused a dismissal under the original contract, and that by continuing to work under the new terms, the employee is in fact working under a new contract. Thus, a claim for unfair dismissal could proceed, even though the employee continues in employment (see *Alcan Extrusions v Yates* [1996] I.R.L.R. 327).

Expiry of Fixed Term Contract

If the employee is employed under a fixed term contract and that contract expires without being renewed, statute deems that the employee has been dismissed (s.95(1)(b) of the ERA 1996).

A fixed term contract is one for which the date of termination of the contract is predetermined, one that will end on the completion of a particular task or agreed amount of work, or a contract which is determinable upon the happening of a future contingent event, e.g. a contract which it has been agreed will terminate if a particular funding source should cease (Fixed-term Employees (Prevention of Less Favourable Treatment) Regulations 2002).

The fact that a fixed term contract may include provision for the contract to be terminated by notice by either party prior to the expiry of the fixed term does not preclude the contract from being a fixed term contract (*Dixon v BBC* [1979] QB 546). Following the introduction of the ERelA 1999, it is no longer possible for employees working on fixed term contracts to waive either their rights to claim unfair dismissal, or their rights to redundancy payments (Fixed-term Worker (Prevention of Less Favourable Treatment) Regulations 2002).

Self-Dismissal

Under the general principle of contract law, if the employee commits a repudiatory breach of contract, that breach will only be effective on the contract once it has been accepted by the innocent party, the employer. Thus, it is the action of the employer which terminates the contract, and thus there is a dismissal (*London Transport Executive v Clarke* [1981] I.C.R. 355). This is not, of course, to suggest that the dismissal is unfair; indeed if the employee has committed a repudiatory breach the dismissal is likely, prima facie, to be fair.

In the case of *Igbo v Johnson Matthey Chemicals Ltd* [1986] I.R.L.R. 215, Mrs Igbo was permitted to take extended holiday on condition that she signed an agreement that should she not return to work on the agreed day her employment would automatically terminate. When she returned from holiday she was ill, so instead of returning to work she sent in a medical certificate. Her employers invoked the agreement and declared her employment terminated. The Court of Appeal, however, held that the automatic termination agreement was invalid as being contrary to s.203(1) of the ERA 1996 which makes void any term of the contract which seeks to exclude or limit any provision of the ERA; and thus a dismissal had taken place.

Frustration
Any contract which is terminated by frustration does not give rise to a dismissal (*Egg Stores (Stamford Hill) Ltd v Leibovici* [1977] I.C.R. 260).

Mutual Consent
Because of the perceived inequality of bargaining powers in the employment relationship, and due to the operation of s.203 of the ERA, termination by mutual consent not resulting in a dismissal will always be difficult to establish particularly in a statutory context. Cases in which the courts have found termination by mutual consent include *SW Strange Ltd v Mann* [1965] 1 All E.R. 1069, *Lipton Ltd v Marlborough* [1979] I.R.L.R. 179, both concerning restraint clauses, *Birch v University of Liverpool* [1985] I.C.R. 470 and *Scott v Coalite Fuels Ltd* [1988] I.C.R. 355 both concerning voluntary early retirement schemes—it should be stressed though that these cases are very much the exception to the rule, and mutual consent is rarely established.

Constructive Dismissal
"an employee is dismissed by his employer if...

the employee terminates the contract under which he is employed (with or without notice) in circumstances in which he is entitled to terminate it without notice by reason of the employer's conduct." (s.95(1)(c) of the ERA 1996).

The question to be asked is, do the actions of the employer constitute a fundamental breach of a term of the contract. If they do, then the employee can claim constructive dismissal.

The leading case, *Western Excavating (ECC) Ltd v Sharp* [1978] QB 761, confirms that the correct test to be applied to determine whether the actions of the employer permit the employee to terminate the contract and claim constructive dismissal, is a "contractual test" not a "reasonableness test." In other words, is the action taken by the employer in accordance with the terms of the contract?—not "has the employer acted reasonably?"

Constructive dismissal may therefore be said to be where the employee terminates the contract due to the employer either committing a fundamental breach of the contract, or evincing clear intentions not to be bound by it.

Although this appears quite straightforward, case law has resulted in some decisions which on the face of it do not appear consistent, and the following principles may be helpful:

(a) an employer cannot be in breach of a contract term by invoking that term, however unreasonable his actions may be (*Western Excavating v Sharp*); but,

(b) by invoking a contract term in an unreasonable manner an employer may be in breach of the fundamental term of "mutual trust and confidence" (*United Bank Ltd v Akhtar* [1989] I.R.L.R. 507).

The duty of mutual trust and confidence has over the years grown in both scope and importance, and for the purposes of constructive dismissal, has included:

(a) Use of abusive language by the employer (*Isle of Wight Tourist Board v Coombes* [1976] I.R.L.R. 413).

(b) Failure to allow an employee reasonable access to a grievance procedure (*WA Goold (Pearmak) Ltd v McConnell* [1995] I.R.L.R. 516).

(c) Refusing to investigate a health and safety complaint (*British Aircraft Corpn v Austin* [1978] I.R.L.R. 332.

(d) Failure to take seriously a complaint of sexual harassment (*Bracebridge Engineering Ltd v Darby* [1990] I.R.L.R. 3).

(e) "Arbitrarily" and "capriciously" refusing an employee a pay rise (*FC Gardiner v Beresford* [1978] I.R.L.R. 63).

(f) Insisting on relocating an employee in the absence of any contractual mobility clause (*Aparau v Iceland Frozen Foods Ltd* [1996] I.R.L.R. 119).

(g) Disproportionate punishment of an employee for a minor offence (*BBC v Beckett* [1983] I.R.L.R. 43).

Although constructive dismissal is usually brought about by a single serious act of the employer, a series of minor incidents may be sufficient (*Woods v WM Car Services (Peterborough) Ltd* [1981] I.C.R. 666, *London Borough of Waltham Forest v Omilaju* [2004] IRLR 35).

Finally, remember that a constructive dismissal is not the same as an unfair dismissal. Usually a finding of constructive dismissal will also lead to the finding of an unfair dismissal, but on occasions the courts have found a constructive dismissal to be fair (*Savoia v Chiltern Herb Farms Ltd* [1981] I.R.L.R. 65).

THE REASON FOR THE DISMISSAL

Statute identifies the potentially fair reasons for dismissal (s.98(2) of the ERA 1996), and to successfully defend a claim of unfair dismissal an employer must initially establish that the reason for dismissal falls within one or more of these categories.

The potentially fair reasons are:

(a) capability or qualifications;
(b) conduct;
(c) redundancy;
(d) contravention of a statute;
(e) some other substantial reason (s.98(1)(b).

Capability or Qualifications

This category may include such issues as skill, aptitude, general ability or ill-health. If the issue is one of incompetence, even one instance may constitute sufficient grounds (*Taylor v Alidair Ltd* [1978] I.R.L.R. 82).

KEY CASE

INTERNATIONAL SPORTS CO LTD V THOMPSON [1980] I.R.L.R. 340
In the last 18 months of employment with International Sports, Ms Thompson was off sick for a total of some five months. Her medical certificates ranged from dizzy spells, to viral infections and flatulence. In agreement with the trade union the company issued a series of warnings to her, and reviewed her medical history which consisted of a series of unrelated, transitory complaints, and finally dismissed her for unsatisfactory performance. She then claimed unfair dismissal.

Held: The dismissal was fair. The company had carried out reasonable investigation into her absences, given her an opportunity to respond, issued warnings, and in the absence of any improvement in her attendance, were justified in dismissing her.

Commentary

Much of the previous case law concerned employees dismissed for absence due to serious and prolonged illness (e.g. *East Lindsey DC v*

Daubney [1977] I.R.L.R. 181). Although this case was considered on the grounds of conduct, in cases such as this, dismissal will normally be on the grounds of capability, since the company would probably not wish to prove that the employee was actually malingering.

Conduct

Conduct has been held to include dishonesty (*British Home Stores v Burchell* [1978] I.R.L.R. 379), fighting at work (*Meakin v Liverpool CC* (EAT/142/00), refusal to obey instructions (*Atkin v Enfield Hospital* [1975] I.R.L.R. 217), breach of health and safety regulations (*Wilcox v Humphries & Glasgow Ltd* [1975] I.R.L.R. 211, etc.

Redundancy

Dismissal on the grounds of redundancy is a potentially fair reason for dismissal. This issue is dealt with more fully in chapter "Redundancy".

Contravention of a Statute

This category would include both the situation in which the circumstance of the employee changes so that his continued employment would become unlawful, e.g. a driver who is subsequently banned by the courts from driving, and also the rare situation where the law changes, making it unlawful to continue to employ someone in a particular job.

Some Other Substantial Reason (SOSR)

This category has been variously termed a "catch-all" or "dustbin" category. It is broad, including such issues as:

(a) Failure by an employee to adapt (*Cresswell v Board of Inland Revenue* [1984] I.C.R. 508).

(b) Clash of personalities (*Treganowan v Robert Knee & Co Ltd* [1975] I.C.R. 405).

(c) Mistaken belief that employee did not have work permit (*Bouchaala v THF Hotels Ltd* [1980] I.C.R. 721).

(d) Failure by employee to disclose medical history when asked at interview (*O'Brien v Prudential Assurance Co Ltd* [1979] I.R.L.R. 140).

(e) Refusal of an employee to accept a new contract term which the employer held "necessary" (*RS Components v Irwin* [1973] I.C.R. 535).

(f) Pressure from a third party (*Scott Packaging Ltd v Patterson* [1978] IRLR 465, *Saunders v Scottish National Camps Association* [1980] I.R.L.R. 174).

(g) Refusal of an employee to accept a drop in wages from £130 to £90 per week negotiated with the trade union (*Sycamore v H Myer & Co Ltd* [1976] I.R.L.R. 84).

The list is by no means exclusive.

Automatically Unfair Reasons
Certain reasons for dismissal (or for selection for redundancy) are automatically unfair.

Assertion of Statutory Right (s.104 of the ERA 1996)
Section 104 ERA makes a dismissal automatically unfair if the reason, or principle reason for it is that the employee had brought proceedings against the employer to enforce a "relevant statutory right". Such rights are any of the rights contained in ERA for which the remedy is via a complaint to an employment tribunal, the right to a minimum notice period, and rights relating to deductions from pay, trade union activities and time off contained in Trade Union and Labour Relations (Consolidation) Act 1992. There is no minimum qualifying period necessary to bring a claim.

Pregnancy and Maternity (s.99 of the ERA 1996)
Dismissal of a worker on the grounds of pregnancy is automatically unfair, there is no qualifying period necessary to bring a claim, and probably no defence available to the employer (but see *Webb v EMO Air Cargo (UK) Ltd* [1995] I.R.L.R. 645).

Trade Union Membership or Non-membership (s.137 of the TULR(C)A 1992)
It is automatically unfair to dismiss a worker for joining, being a member of, refusing to join or refusing to remain a member of a trade union. There is no minimum qualifying period necessary to bring such a claim.

Dismissal of Striking Employees (ERelA 1999)
The dismissal of an employee for taking part in official industrial action is automatically unfair if it occurs within the first eight weeks of such participation. A dismissal after that period may also be unfair if the employer fails to take reasonable steps to resolve the dispute.

Employee Representatives (s.103 of the ERA 1996)
Dismissal of an employees representative (under Ch.II, Pt IV of the TULR(C)A 1992) or a candidate for election to such a position is automatically unfair if the principle reason for such a dismissal relates to the activities of the role.

Health and Safety (s.100 of the ERA 1996)

Particular protection is afforded by s.100 of the ERA 1996 to health and safety representatives and members of health and safety committees, and also to workers in companies in which there is no health and safety representative or committee, to make automatically unfair any dismissal on the grounds that the employee was carrying out health and safety duties. No qualifying period is necessary to bring such a claim.

Sunday Work (s.101 of the ERA 1996)

Certain groups of shop workers are protected against dismissal for refusal to work on Sundays (Pt IV of the ERA 1996).

Transfer of Undertakings (TUPE 2006)

Dismissal by reason of the transfer or for a reason connected with the transfer which is not an "economic technical or organisational reason" will be automatically unfair.

Trustees of Occupational Pension Schemes (s.102 of the ERA 1996)

Protected if the reason or principle reason for the dismissal is that the employee performed any function as such a trustee.

THE FAIRNESS OF THE DISMISSAL

Once it has been shown that the applicant is qualified to make a claim, that a dismissal has taken place, and that the employer has put forward a potentially fair reason for the dismissal, only then is it necessary to consider the fairness of the dismissal.

Statute states that:

"the determination of the question whether the dismissal is fair or unfair (having regard to the reason shown by the employer) depends on whether in the circumstances (including the size and administrative resources of the employer's undertaking) the employer acted reasonably or unreasonably in treating it as a sufficient reason for dismissing the employee, and shall be determined in accordance with equity and the substantial merits of the case." (s.98(4) of the ERA 1996).

The fairness of the dismissal may be divided into two broad headings, both of which must be satisfied in order to prove a fair dismissal: the band of reasonable responses, and procedural fairness.

Band of Reasonable Responses

"[The] tribunal must consider the reasonableness of the employer's conduct, not simply whether they (the members of the industrial tribunal) consider the dismissal to be fair; in judging the reasonableness of the employer's conduct an industrial tribunal must not substitute its decision as to what was the right course to adopt for that of the employer; in many, though not all, cases there is a band of reasonable responses to the employee's conduct within which one employer might reasonably take one view, another quite reasonably take another; the function of the industrial tribunal ... is to determine whether in the particular circumstances of each case the decision to dismiss the employee fell within the band of reasonable responses which a reasonable employer might have adopted." (*Iceland Frozen Foods v Jones* [1983] I.C.R. 17, per Browne-Wilkinson J.).

Thus in summary, the tribunal must not ask, "What would we have done in that situation?", but instead, in effect, "Could a reasonable employer have done what was done?", if so, at this stage, the dismissal will be fair (for an example see the recent case of *Jobcentre plus DWP v Graham* (2011) UKEAT/0610/10).

Obviously, the range of reasonable responses may be very broad, and have, in the past, included:

(a) The dismissal of an attendant at a boys' camp solely on the grounds of his homosexuality (*Saunders v Scottish National Camps Association* [1980] I.R.L.R. 174).

(b) The dismissal of a rail steward of 14 years' service for having in his possession food, in contravention of a regulation prohibiting employees engaging in business on their own account (*British Railways Board v Jackson* [1994] I.R.L.R. 235).

(c) The dismissal of both employees where it was believed that one was guilty of theft, but it could not be ascertained which (*Monie v Coral Racing Ltd* [1981] I.C.R. 109).

Thus, the range of reasonable responses to a situation of, say, horseplay at work could range from an informal rebuke, a formal warning, to dismissal. Each of these responses may be considered fair.

Doubt was cast on the band of reasonable responses test by the EAT in the case of *Haddon v Van Den Bergh Foods Ltd* [1999] I.R.L.R. 672, who considered that because of the ease with which the test may be satisfied by an employer, the test was "a test of perversity". These views were, however firmly overruled by the Court of Appeal in the joined cases of *Post Office v Foley*; *HSBC (formerly Midland Bank) v Madden* [2000] I.R.L.R. 827 who confirmed that the band of reasonable responses test should continue to be applied in accordance with binding case law.

Procedural Fairness

It is possible for a dismissal for a fair reason, which is within the range of reasonable responses, to be found unfair if it fails the test of procedural fairness. ACAS have a Code of Practice which, whilst not having the force of law, may be relied upon as a blueprint for an employer's own disciplinary code. The Code lays down a system of warnings for misconduct etc., and follows the principles of natural justice. If an employer abides by the ACAS Code it is most unlikely if not almost impossible that a tribunal would hold that a dismissal was procedurally unfair.

The House of Lords in the case of *Polkey v AE Dayton Services Ltd* [1988] I.C.R. 142, stressed the importance of following an agreed procedure in disciplinary hearings, holding that a failure to follow such procedure was likely to result in a finding of unfair dismissal, unless "the employer could reasonably have concluded in the light of circumstances known at the time of dismissal that consultation or warning would be utterly useless." A finding that a dismissal is unfair on procedural grounds only may result in a tribunal making a discretionary deduction from the amount of compensation that would otherwise have been awarded; such reductions in compensation are termed "*Polkey* reductions"— for a recent example see *Frew v Springboig St John's School* (UKEATS/0052/10).

Generally, in assessing the fairness of a dismissal the tribunal may only take into account facts known to the employer at the time of dismissal (*W Devis & Sons Ltd v Atkins* [1977] A.C. 931), but the House of Lords in *West Midlands Co-operative Society Ltd v Tipton* [1986] A.C. 536 held that facts arising out of a post-dismissal appeal may also be taken into account by the tribunal. The effect of this is that if an employee is denied an appeal to which he is contractually entitled, the dismissal will almost certainly be unfair.

A drawing together of many of the principles of unfair dismissal may be seen from the case of *British Home Stores v Burchell* [1978] I.R.L.R. 379 in which the employee was dismissed because the employer believed she was stealing on a staff discount scheme.

Ms Burchell fulfilled the requirements necessary for her to make a claim. The reason put forward for her dismissal was conduct, her alleged theft.

The EAT laid down a three part test:

(a) that the employer honestly held the belief,

(b) that the employer had reasonable grounds on which to sustain that belief,

(c) that the employer had carried out as much investigation as was reasonable in all the circumstances.

It is important to note that the question for the tribunal did not concern the guilt or innocence of Ms Burchell, but the question of whether in view of the facts as they were known to the employer at the time, the employer acted reasonably both in the decision and the manner of her dismissal. For a further consideration of the Burchell test see, for example, the case of *Boys and Girls Welfare Society v McDonald* [1996] I.R.L.R. 129.

There is a right (s.10 Employment Relations Act 1999) for the employee to be accompanied at a disciplinary or grievance hearing by a co-worker or trade union official. In cases where the employee livelihood may be put in jeopardy, legal representation may be allowed in order to avoid a breach of Article 6 ECHR (see dicta from *R (on the application of G) v Governers of X School* [2011] IRLR 756).

Remedies for Unfair Dismissal

The tribunal may award any of three remedies as may be requested by the successful applicant: reinstatement, re-engagement, or compensation.

Reinstatement

Requires the employer to treat the employee as if he had not been dismissed, making good arrears of pay, any increments or improvements in terms and conditions to which the employee would have been entitled, etc.

Re-engagement

Requires the employer to engage the employee on the same or comparable work, on terms and conditions such as the tribunal may require, including such matters as an amount for pay arrears, etc.

The main problem with orders for both reinstatement and re-engagement is that in most cases by this stage the duty of mutual trust and confidence between the employer and the employee will have broken down, making such orders unworkable.

Compensation

May take the form of a basic award computed in the same way as a redundancy payment; a compensatory award to reflect the loss sustained by the applicant due to the dismissal; an additional award should the employer not comply with a reinstatement or re-engagement order; and a special award payable only in cases of trade union membership or health and safety dismissals.

Chapter Checklist

You should now know and understand:

- the basic answer structure to any question on unfair dismissal;

- the relationship between unfair dismissal and wrongful dismissal;

- the relationship between employee status and unfair dismissal;

- issues of continuity of employment;

- how to identify a dismissal;

- the potentially fair reasons for dismissal;

- the potentially unfair reasons for dismissal;

- the band of reasonable responses;

- issues of procedural fairness;

- remedies available to the successful complainant.

Figure 5 Unfair Dismissal

Step 1 Can the applicant claim?
    a) Is the applicant an employee?
    b) Does he belong to an excluded group?
    c) Does he have a minimum of 1 year's continuity of employment?
    d) Is the application made within the permitted time scale?

Step 2 Can a dismissal be identified?

Step 3 Is the reason for the dismissal one of the potentially fair reasons under s.98 ERA?

Step 4 The fairness of the dismissal
    a) "Band of reasonable responses" test
    b) Procedural fairness

Remedies
    a) Reinstatement
    b) Re-engagement
    c) Compensation

QUESTION AND ANSWER

The Question

Harry and Ian both worked for XCo Ltd in their warehouse. It was common knowledge that they did not get on with each other, and on one occasion the personnel manager had given both of them a "first and final warning", when an argument between them had resulted in an angry exchange, threats and an amount of "pushing and shoving."

Yesterday afternoon the personnel manager called both of them into his office following complaints from another worker that "it sounds as if they are killing each other in there!"

Harry had a cut lip and a bruised hand, Ian had a black eye. When questioned, both were sullen; Harry mumbled "He started it," whereas Ian claimed he had walked into a door.

The personnel manager told them that fighting constituted gross misconduct, and in any case they had both had a previous warning; consequently both were summarily dismissed and must leave the premises immediately.

Discuss any likely action by Harry and/or Ian.

Suggested points for consideration

The two courses of action open to Harry and Ian would be actions for either unfair dismissal or wrongful dismissal.

Unfair Dismissal
(a) Can the applicant claim? Both would appear to be employees. Neither belong to an excluded group. Although we are not told, it may be assumed that both have a minimum of one year's service. The claim must be brought within three months.
(b) Can a dismissal be identified? Yes—both have been summarily dismissed.
(c) The reason for the dismissal. The reason for the dismissal is the conduct of the employees, i.e. fighting. "Conduct" is a potentially fair reason for dismissal under s.98(2)(b) of the ERA 1996.
(d) The fairness of the dismissal.

(a) Did the actions of the employer fall within the band of reasonable responses which a reasonable employer might have adopted (*Iceland*

Frozen Foods v Jones)? In this case, dismissal of employees for fighting may well amount to a reasonable response.

(b) Procedural fairness:

It may be helpful to apply the test from *BHS v Burchell*:
(1) that the employer honestly held the belief;
(2) that the employer had reasonable grounds on which to sustain that belief; and
(3) that the employer had carried out a reasonable investigation.

In this case, the test is probably satisfied. The employer believed that the employees had been fighting, there were reasonable grounds for that belief, and since it appears that there were no witnesses, it is difficult to know what further investigation could have been made.

However, one important issue remains; is a summary dismissal justified in the circumstances? This would depend on several factors, is there a contract term stating that fighting constitutes gross misconduct, what were the specific terms of the warning given, when was the warning given, how has the company reacted to other instances of fighting (*Meakin v Liverpool City Council*)?

Wrongful Dismissal

An action for wrongful dismissal generally concerns only whether the correct contract notice period has been given (*Addis*) and not the reason for the dismissal as such. In this case the tribunal would need to decide whether the company was contractually entitled to dismiss the employees without notice (*Sinclair v Neighbour*).

Redundancy

12

LEGISLATION HIGHLIGHTER

EMPLOYMENT RIGHTS ACT 1996 SECTION 139

Redundancy is considered in some academic courses and text books as a separate and distinct issue; in fact, of course, redundancy is merely one of the potentially fair reasons for dismissal—outlined in s.98(1)(b) of the ERA 1996 although certain distinctive rules and legislation apply to it.

Lord Denning's explanation of redundancy may be a helpful starting point:

"a worker of long standing is now recognised as having an accrued right in his job; and his right gains in value with the years. So much so that if the job is shut down he is entitled to compensation for loss of the job...The worker gets a redundancy payment. It is not unemployment pay...Even if he gets another job straightaway, he nevertheless is entitled to full redundancy payment. It is, in a real sense, compensation for long service. No man gets it unless he has been employed for at least two years by the employer; and then the amount of it depends solely upon his age and length of service." (*Lloyd v Brassey* [1969] 2 QB 98).

Section 139(1) of the ERA 1996 states:

"For the purposes of this Act an employee who is dismissed shall be taken to be dismissed by reason of redundancy if the dismissal is wholly or mainly attributable to:

(a) the fact that his employer has ceased or intends to cease—
   i) to carry on the business for the purposes of which the employee was employed by him; or
   ii) to carry on that business in the place where the employee was so employed; or

(b) the fact that the requirements of that business—
   i) for employees to carry out work of a particular kind; or
   ii) for employees to carry out work of a particular kind in the place where the employee was employed by the employer,

have ceased or diminished or are expected to cease or diminish."

Although at first glance this appears fairly straightforward, there are in particular two areas of concern: what is meant by "work of a particular kind", and what is the "place of work"?

Work of a Particular Kind

Contract test v Job Function test v Statutory test   Different approaches have been adopted by the courts in the past. The earlier "job function test" called on the court to consider whether the overall function of the role, rather than the specific work detailed in the employment contract, had changed. If the function had remained then any dismissal would not have been on the grounds of redundancy.

An example of this can be seen in the case of *North Riding Garages v Butterwick* [1967] 2 QB 56, in which an employee of 30 years' service had worked his way up to workshop manager although he still spent much of his time working as a hands-on mechanic. New owners took over and required the workshop manager to concentrate more of his time on sales and paperwork, which he was unable to do satisfactorily. After some months he was dismissed, and he claimed redundancy. In holding that he was not redundant, the court stated that employees have a duty to adapt to new methods and techniques, and only if the new methods alter the nature of the work required may they be redundant. In the case of Mr Butterwick his function as workshop manager remained, thus he was not redundant.

The later "contract test" required the court to consider the range of work the employee could be called upon to perform under their contract—rather than merely the actual work the employee has been doing—and if this work had diminished or ceased the employee would be redundant. This may be illustrated by the case of *Nelson v BBC* [1980] I.C.R. 100, in which the employee was employed as a producer and editor for the BBC. He had worked for much of his career in the Caribbean Service, and when this service was closed down the question arose as to whether Mr Nelson was redundant.

The Court of Appeal held that although there was a diminution in the specific work Mr Nelson had actually been doing, there was no such diminution in the work of producers and editors generally, which was the work he was contracted to do; thus Mr Nelson was not redundant.

The third, and current, approach—a "statutory test"—was introduced by the EAT in the case of *Safeway Stores Plc v Burrell* [1997] I.R.L.R. 200, as follows:

(a) Was the employee dismissed?

(b) If so, was there a diminution or cessation in the requirements of the employer's business for employees (not the employee) to carry out work of a particular kind, or an expectation of such in the future?

(c) If so, was the dismissal of the employee caused wholly or mainly by that state of affairs?

The terms of the employee's contract of employment are not relevant for consideration at the second stage; they will only become relevant, if at all, at the third stage.

Application of this "statutory test" allows for the principle of "bumping" whereby an employee may be made redundant, not because his own job is redundant, but because his job has been filled by another employee who would otherwise themselves have been made redundant

Although this "statutory test" was itself doubted by a differently constituted EAT in the case of *Church v West Lancashire NHS Trust* [1998] I.R.L.R. 4, who stated that the proper test is a "sensible blend" of the contractual and functional approaches, the House of Lords in *Murray v Foyle Meats* [1999] I.R.L.R. 562 has confirmed that the "statutory" test is to be applied, and that both the "contract" test and the "job function" test are themselves redundant and should not be followed. Their Lordships stated that if a dismissal is attributable to a redundancy situation, the dismissal will be by way of redundancy.

This important case both clarifies, and indeed simplifies, the situation and also impliedly confirms the lawfulness of bumped redundancies.

Place of Work

The problem faced by the court has been to decide whether the inclusion of a mobility clause in the employee's contract should be the deciding factor in defining the place of work with reference to redundancy.

If a purely contractual approach is taken, and if the employee's contract contains a general mobility clause, an employer may avoid a redundancy situation by offering the employee work in any location—which considering the case of *Western Excavating* (see "constructive dismissal") would perhaps appear to be the correct approach.

However, although in the case of *O'Brien v Associated Fire Alarms Ltd* [1968] 1 W.L.R. 1916 the court adopted a contractual test, in the later case of *Bass Leisure Ltd v Thomas* [1994] I.R.L.R. 104 the EAT instead applied a geographical approach, looking at where the applicant had actually worked, rather than at where he could have worked. This has been supported by the Court of Appeal decision in *High Table Ltd v Horst* [1997] I.R.L.R. 513 which favoured the factual or geographical approach to "place of work". It is presently arguable whether, following *Murray v Foyle Meats*, this is still a contentious issue.

HIGH TABLE LTD V HORST [1997] I.R.L.R. 513

Ms Horst had worked for High Table, a catering services company, as a waitress for a number of years at the premises of one of their clients, Hill Samuel, in the City of London. Following a down turn in the business between High Table and Hill Samuel in 1993, Ms Horst was made redundant.

She argued that since her employment contract contained an express mobility clause—which purported to allow the employer to transfer staff on a temporary or permanent basis to any location—her "place of work" was at any of her employer's clients, and not just at Hill Samuels. She maintained that she could and should have been offered work elsewhere, thus was not redundant, and claimed unfair dismissal.

Held: The Court of Appeal rejected her argument, coming down in favour of a factual approach, and stating:

"If an employee has worked in only one location under his contract of employment ... it defies common sense to widen the extent of the place where he was so employed, merely because of the existence of a mobility clause. Of course, the refusal by the employee to obey a lawful requirement under the contract of employment to move may constitute a valid reason for dismissal, but issues of dismissal, redundancy and reasonableness in the actions of an employer should be kept distinct." per Peter Gibson L.J.

Commentary

Presumably therefore, place of work is factual. Even if the employee has a mobility clause in the contract, if there is a down turn of work in one particular location in which the employer has always worked, this may constitute redundancy. On the other hand, should the employer choose instead to transfer the employee to another location, rather than declare him redundant, then following Western Excavating, this will be lawful; unless either the reason for the transfer or the manner of the transfer breach the implied duty of trust and confidence (*United Bank v Akhtar*), in which case it may lead to unfair dismissal.

Who is Eligible?

The claimant must firstly be an employee, they must have been dismissed (s.136 of the ERA 1996), and they must have a minimum of two years' continuous employment (s.155 of the ERA 1996) (cf one year requirement for unfair dismissal) on the "relevant date" (s.145 of the ERA 1996)—the relevant date being either the date on which notice expires, or in the case of termination without notice, the date on which termination takes effect. However, in certain circumstances, where the minimum notice period required by s.86 of the ERA 1996 would if given have expired at a later date, that later date will be the relevant date (s.145(5) of the ERA 1996).

In addition, certain categories are excluded from redundancy rights including those dismissed for misconduct or industrial action, (s.140 of the ERA 1996),

Continuity of Employment

As stated above, to be eligible for redundancy an employee must have a minimum of two years' continuous employment. In certain instances continuity of employment will be preserved, even though the employee apparently changes employers:

(a) Associated Employers. The business of the employer together with the business of his associated employers will be treated as one (s.139(2) of the ERA 1996), and companies are treated as associated if either one has control of the other, or both are controlled by a third party (s.231 of the ERA 1996).

(b) Transfer of Business. If a trade, business or undertaking is transferred the period of employment at the time of the transfer counts as a period of employment with the transferee (s.218(2) of the ERA 1996).

In the case of the sale of a business this normally means that there must be the transfer of the business as a going concern—probably including the goodwill—and not merely the sale of individual assets (*Melon v Hector Powe Ltd* [1981] I.C.R. 43).

Procedure

In order to ensure that the redundancy may not be held to amount to an unfair dismissal, it is important that the employer should follow a procedure of good industrial practice, such as was laid down in the case of *Williams v Compair Maxam Ltd* [1982] I.C.R. 156:

(a) The employer should give as much warning as possible.

(b) The employer should consult with the trade union, particularly regarding selection procedure.

(c) The selection procedure should be objective.

(d) The employer should ensure that the selection procedure is followed.

(e) The employer should seek to offer alternative employment.

In relation to the guidelines from Compair, the following points should also be considered:

(a) In situations where there is a proposal to make more than 20 redundancies the employer has a statutory duty to consult with the union or other appropriate representatives (s.188 of the TULR(C)A 1992). Note, however, that the employer's duty is to consult, not to agree, with the union—the final decision is the employer's.

(b) Following the introduction of s.98A of the ERA 1996, the failure by an employer to follow an agreed procedure, other than the statutory procedures, will not necessarily make the redundancy dismissal unfair.

(c) There is no clear authority on how closely the tribunal may examine the procedure adopted for redundancy selection. Certainly, the more transparent the system (e.g. LIFO—last in first out), the more likely it is that the tribunal will not question it (*British Aerospace Plc v Green* [1995] I.C.R. 1006).

(d) Certain selections for redundancy will be automatically unfair, e.g. trade union activities (s.153 of the TULR(C)A), pregnancy, etc.

(e) If the employer makes an offer of suitable alternative employment to an employee before the end of his employment, there are two possible consequences:

   i)   if the employee accepts the offer, then subject to a four week trial period, there will be no dismissal; or

   ii) if the employee unreasonably refuses the offer, he will be barred from claiming a redundancy payment.

The question then arises, what constitutes "suitable alternative employment"?

In the case of *Taylor v Kent CC* [1969] 2 QB 560, a head teacher whose school was merged with another was offered a post as supply teacher, but at his old salary. The court agreed that the demotion in status was sufficient to make the new position unsuitable.

Likewise, generally a drop in pay or earning potential will make a new position unsuitable, but since suitability is a question of fact for the tribunal, this need not always be the case (see *Sheppard v NCB* [1966] 1 K.I.R. 101).

The second issue for the tribunal is whether the refusal of the offer is unreasonable. Here the test is subjective, and the tribunal may take into account such personal factors as health, family commitments, etc. (*John Fowler Ltd v Parkin* [1975] I.R.L.R. 89).

Compensation

Redundancy compensation is calculated as follows:

(a) For each year worked over the age of 18 but under the age of 22, half a week's gross pay.

(b) For each year worked over the age of 22 but under the age of 41, one week's gross pay.

(c) For each year worked over the age of 41 but under normal retirement, one and a half week's pay.

A maximum of 20 years of employment can be taken into account (s.162(3) of the ERA 1996), also be aware of the statutory maximum amount for the basic calculation of "a week's pay."

Chapter Checklist

You should now know and understand:

- how to identify a redundancy;

- fair redundancy procedure;

- the compensation available to redundant workers.

QUESTION AND ANSWER

The Question

Maureen has been employed by XCo for just over two years, working in the sales department. The previous holder of the post, Nora, has been with the company for over 20 years and is now in the customer services department. The company has just announced that due to a shortage of new orders the customer services department is being closed, Nora is being transferred back to the sales department, and Maureen is being made redundant at the end of the month.

Advise Maureen of any claim she may have against XCo.

Suggested points for consideration

The question concerns redundancy, and in particular the practice known as "bumping". The starting point for any answer should be s.139(1) of the ERA 1996, followed by consideration of the three tests applied by the courts: the contract test, the job function test, and the statutory test. Of particular relevance is the test from *Safeway v Burrell*, which allows for the principle of "bumping", and this is supported by *Murray v Foyle Meats*.

Assuming that the company follow a similar procedure to that laid down in *Williams v Compair*, application of *Safeway* would suggest that Maureen has no claim against redundancy.

Transfer of Undertakings

TRANSFER OF UNDERTAKINGS (PROTECTION OF EMPLOYMENT)
REGULATIONS 2006

Common Law Position

Since the common law holds that the contract of employment is a personal contract and not an asset of the company as such, it follows that the sale or transfer of a business would have the effect of terminating the contract, rather than transferring it. It is uncertain what effect the common law would have on the individual contracts of employment; they may on occasion be determined automatically without breach (*Re General Rolling Stock Co* (1866) L.R. 1 Eq. 346), or they may be terminated by breach giving rise to a claim for wrongful dismissal (*Nokes v Doncaster Amalgamated Collieries Ltd* [1940] A.C. 1014).

However, since the intervention of statute through redundancy, unfair dismissal and more recently regulations governing transfers of undertakings, the common law position has little relevance in practice.

Transfer of Undertakings (Protection of Employment) Regulations 2006 (TUPE)

The original TUPE Regulations were introduced to implement **EC Directive 77/ 187 (the Acquired Rights Directive)** and have since both been amended and given rise to amendments of other legislation. Although the regulations are fairly complex—and certainly much case law has been generated both by the regulations and the Directive—the main thrust of the regulations is contained in regs 3 and 4:

Regulation 3 defines a "relevant transfer" as "a transfer of an undertaking, business or part of an undertaking or business situated immediately before the transfer in the United Kingdom to another person where there is a transfer of an economic entity which retains its identity." The Regulations also cover "service provision changes" (see for example the case of *Suzen*), both public and private undertakings—whether or not they are operating for gain, but exclude mere administrative reorganisations of public administrative authorities.

Regulation 4 deals with the effect of relevant transfers on contracts of employment and states that the "transfer shall not operate so as to terminate the contract of employment of any person employed by the transferor". Paragraph 5 of the same Regulation does however allow the employer to agree to vary such contracts of employment if the sole reason for such variation is "an economic, technical or organisational reason entailing changes in the workforce".

Thus the contracts of employment of all employees of the transferor are automatically transferred to the transferee on the same terms and conditions as were previously enjoyed by the employees. If an employee objects to his contract being transferred he is entitled to refuse, but the effect of this is to terminate the contract without a dismissal taking place (reg.4(7)).

Only if the proposed transfer would result in a significant and detrimental change to the employee may the employee terminate the contract and claim unfair dismissal via constructive dismissal (reg.4(9)). It was not firmly established whether such a claim would lie against the transferee as well as the transferor (*Unicorn Consultancy Services Ltd v Westbrook* [2000] I.R.L.R. 80; cf. *Mitie Services Ltd v French* [2002] I.R.L.R. 512) since art 3.1 of the Directive allows for joint liability, but the 2006 regulations state that all liabilities pass to the transferee at the time of the transfer (*Bernadone v Pall Mall Services* [2000] IRLR 487).

"Undertaking"

TUPE defines an "undertaking" as including any trade or business, but this definition has been widened, following the case of *Dr Sophie Redmond Stichting v Bartol* [1992] I.R.L.R. 366, to include non-commercial organisations, for example charities. However, "activities involving the exercise of public authority" are not included (*Henke v Gemeinde Schierke und Verwaltungsgemeinschaft Brocken* [1996] I.R.L.R. 701). Regulation 3(5) of the 2006 Regulations confirms that TUPE does not apply to either reorganisations within public authorities or transfers of functions between public authorities.

"Relevant Transfer"

The ECJ in *Suzen v Zehnacker Gebaudereinigung GmbH Krankenhausservice* [1997] I.R.L.R. 255 held that the transfer must relate to "a stable economic entity whose activity is not limited to performing one specific works contract"; and by so doing apparently overruled the authority of cases such as *Schmidt v Spar—und Leihkasse* [1994] I.R.L.R. 302 which had held that the transfer of a single individual employee to a sub-contractor could amount to a relevant transfer. It is possible to view *Suzen* as suggesting that the courts will look to find a transfer of physical assets rather than merely a transfer of labour before holding that the transfer is a "relevant transfer" and falls within the ambit of the Directive and regulations—and this view was supported by the ECJ in *Oy Liikenne Ab v Liskojarvi* [2001] I.R.L.R. 171—although such a view would appear to be contrary to s.3 of the 2006 Regulations.

This is not, however, to suggest that a transfer may take place merely on the sale of an undertaking's assets. The ECJ in the case of *Spijkers v Gebroeders Benedik Abattoir CV* [1986] 2 C.M.L.R. 296 stated that a transfer will only take place within the meaning of the Directive if the entity in question retains its identity, in other words if the organisation is transferred as a going concern, probably including goodwill. In the recent case of *Klar-enberg v Ferrotron Technologies GmbH* [2009] IRLR 301 the ECJ held that TUPE could still apply if there was a "functional link between the various elements of production transferred", and that the question would be for the national courts to decide.

Other points of note include:

(a) The Directive and the regulations apply both to the contracting-out of services and to the process of compulsory competitive tendering (CCT) (*Rask v ISS Kantineservice* [1993] I.R.L.R. 133, but consider the possible limitations imposed by *Suzen*).

(b) Neither the Directive nor the regulations consider as relevant transfers changes of ownership brought about by share purchases.

(c) Some of the post-*Suzen* case law appears confusing and contradictory. The Court of Appeal in the case of *ECM (Vehicle Delivery Service) Ltd v Cox* [1999] I.C.R. 1162 held that the economic entity which was transferred was a contract to do work and the work done under that contract, rather than any tangible assets. It may be that the court in this case was particularly influenced by the fact that the company involved specifically attempted to avoid the application of TUPE.

Dismissal of Employees

TUPE reg.4 provides that if an employee is dismissed either before or after a relevant transfer, and the reason or principle reason for that dismissal is the transfer, that dismissal will be regarded as unfair.

However, reg.4 then allows either the transferor or the transferee the complete defence of "some other substantial reason" for the dismissal on the grounds of "economic, technical or organisational" (ETO) reasons. This may be taken to mean that in such a situation the employee would not even be entitled to a redundancy payment, however the EAT in the case of *Gor-ictree v Jenkinson* [1985] I.C.R. 51 held that the ETO defence is not synonymous with the s.98 of the ERA 1996 SOSR, and thus entitlement to a redundancy payment would not be lost.

The following points should also be noted:

(a) The transferee cannot escape liability by arranging that the transferor should dismiss surplus staff before the transfer takes place. In the case of *Litster v Forth Dry Dock and Engg Co Ltd* [1989] I.C.R. 341 the respondent company was in receivership and agreed to dismiss the workforce before the transfer took place, so as to make the transfer more attractive to the transferee by attempting to avoid for the transferee any liability under TUPE, (the transferor being in receivership and with the debtors having realised their security, there were insufficient assets to meet the transferor's liability for unfair dismissal or redundancy claims). The House of Lords adopted a purposive approach to the legislation however, and stated that the regulation should be read as if the words "or would have been so employed if he had not been unfairly dismissed..." had been inserted after "...a person so employed immediately before the transfer..." (words which are now included in reg.4(3) TUPE 2006). Thus the dismissed employees were brought within the scope of the regulations, and the transferee became responsible for their dismissal.

(b) Liability for unfair dismissal may be automatically passed from the transferor to the transferee, even though the transferee may not have been party to any of the prior discussions (*Thompson v Walon Car Delivery and BRS Automotive Ltd* [1997] I.R.L.R. 343).

KEY CASE

BERRIMAN V DELABOLE SLATE LTD [1985] I.R.L.R. 305
Mr Berriman's employers sold their business as a going concern to Delabole Slate, who wished to bring the terms of the new employees into line with their existing staff. This would result in a decrease in guaranteed pay for Mr Berriman, who rejected the offer, left and claimed unfair dismissal.

Held: Initially the tribunal held that the dismissal was for an "economic, technical or organisational reason", and did not therefore constitute unfair dismissal.

Both the EAT and the Court of Appeal took a different view. They held that the reason for the dismissal was that the new employer wished to change employment terms and conditions of the transferred staff, and that "the reason itself does not involve any change either in the number or the functions of the workforce".

Commentary

The court appears to have adopted a purposive approach, and at first glance this decision appears to afford considerable protection to transferred workers. However, the question that needs to be asked is for how long could this situation continue—at what point would a change in the transferred employee's terms cease to be as a result of the transfer, and become a potentially fair SOSR?

Consultation over Transfers

There is a duty under TUPE to both inform and consult with employees representatives prior to any relevant transfer. The grounds for consultation include the timing of the transfer, the reasons for it and the legal, economic and social implications.

Employee representatives may be either trade union representatives or non-union worker representatives, perhaps elected solely for the consultation process.

KEY CASE

BETTS V BRINTEL HELICOPTERS LTD AND KLM ERA HELICOPTERS (UK) LTD [1997] I.R.L.R. 361

Brintel had provided helicopter services under three contracts to Shell (UK) Ltd. When the contracts expired, Brintel were re-awarded two of them, but the third was won by KLM. KLM did not take over any of Brintel's helicopters or staff, nor did they use the same flying base. Although some of Brintel's staff were re-deployed within Brintel's other operations, some, including Betts, were not. Betts claimed unfair dismissal.

The question for the court was whether there had been a transfer of undertakings between KLM and Brintel, if so, the dismissal may well have been unfair under TUPE.

Held: The Court of Appeal followed the recently decided case of *Suzen*, and held that there had been no transfer. It argued that although the operation of the third contract by Brintel had amounted to an undertaking or economic entity, that undertaking had not been transferred. They reasoned that since very few of Brintel's assets had passed to KLM, there was insufficient evidence to show that the undertaking had retained its identity in the hands of KLM.

Commentary

In this case there is evidence that, had Betts and others not claimed for unfair dismissal, they may well have been engaged by KLM, arguably this should have strengthened the case that a transfer had taken place. However, the court needed to give full consideration to the recently given judgement of the ECJ in the case of *Suzen*; one potential effect of *Suzen* is that transfers may be more difficult to prove the more labour intensive a business becomes, since *Suzen* places considerable emphasis on the transfer of physical assets in proving a genuine transfer of an economic entity.

Chapter Checklist

You should now know and understand:

- the scope of the regulations;
- the application of the regulations.

QUESTION AND ANSWER

The Question

Mrs Oswald has worked for XCo since 2000. She worked from home filling envelopes, on average working some 20 hours per week. Some weeks there was almost no work for her, in others she worked over 40 hours. The company have always treated her as self-employed, paying her gross, and not providing holiday or sick pay.

Two months ago XCo sold its business as a going concern to YCo Ltd, who have a policy of not using home workers. Consequently, for the past two months Mrs Oswald has received no work.

Advise Mrs Oswald

Suggested points for consideration

If Mrs Oswald is self-employed she will have no claim against either XCo or YCo. However, if she is an employee, under TUPE her dismissal by YCo is automatically unfair, although the company may have a defence under ETO reasons, alternatively, the failure to provide her with an opportunity to earn wages would amount to a breach of contract (*Devonald v Rosser*).

To determine Mrs Oswald's status apply dicta from *Nethermere v Gardiner* and *Carmichael v National Power, etc.*

Restraint of Trade

14

A distinction must be drawn between competition during the employment relationship, and competition once the relationship has ended.

Competition whilst Employed

Competition during the life of the employment contract will usually fall foul of the implied duty of fidelity imposed on the employee, and amount to a breach of contract by the employee; it may also enable the employer to obtain an injunction against a third party, restraining them from employing the employee whilst the original contract is in force (*Hivac Ltd v Park Royal Scientific Instruments Ltd* [1946] Ch. 169).

The situation is less certain in the case of an employee who is working for an employer only on a part time basis. Whilst in theory the employer could seek an injunction to prevent the employee working elsewhere during the period of his contract, since the granting of an injunction is an equitable remedy and thus discretionary, and since the employee is only contracted on a part time basis, it is unlikely that a court would be willing to comply in most cases. Perhaps if the contract reflected the need for particular fidelity, either through a specific express clause or in the level of salary paid, an injunction may be granted.

Garden Leave

Although an order of specific performance may not be granted to oblige an employee to work for a particular employer (s.236 of the TULR(C)A 1992), in many cases companies are able to write long notice periods into contracts and then enforce the notice period without requiring the employee to actually attend for work. The effect of this is that the employee is paid to stay at home—"garden leave"—and may be legally restrained from taking up other employment during that notice period (*Evening Standard Co Ltd v Henderson* [1987] I.C.R. 588). Such clauses are now common in the contracts of senior employees, they enable an employer to protect all of their business interests for a period of several months should an employee decide to join a competitor.

In more recent years though the courts have adopted a less consistent approach to the issue of garden leave. Although in *GFI Group Inc v Eaglestone* [1994] I.R.L.R. 119 an injunction was granted prohibiting an employee from taking up new employment before his notice period had expired, in the case of *William Hill Org Ltd v Tucker* [1998] I.R.L.R. 313, the Court of Appeal both declined to grant a similar injunction and doubted that in such situations an injunction enforcing garden leave should be granted, but rather the employer should seek to rely upon a restrictive covenant within the employment contract.

Restrictive Covenants

A restrictive covenant is an express term of the contract of employment which purports to extend beyond the life of the contract and restrain the employee from working, post contract; for a particular employer; in a particular industry; in a particular role; or in a particular location or geographical area, for an agreed length of time. Such terms are common in many employment contracts; their purpose being to prevent ex-employees from taking knowledge, skills, information, etc. to a competitor. However, the doctrine of restraint of trade holds that, prima facie, such agreements are void. The court will only uphold a restrictive covenant if it is satisfied that the employer has a legitimate proprietary interest to protect, such as a trade secret, a particular manufacturing process, a client base or, perhaps, its existing employees; and then only for as long as is fair and necessary.

In effect, the court has to balance the right of the ex-employee to work and do business, with the right of the ex-employer to reasonable protection, whilst not offending against the overriding issue of public policy. Whilst it is quite proper that confidential information and trade secrets of various types should be protected, it is equally proper that the individual should be permitted to practice and exercise skills and knowledge legitimately gained.

It should be noted that if the employer repudiates the contract, perhaps through wrongful dismissal, they will not be entitled to rely on a restrictive covenant (*General Billposting v Atkinson* [1909] AC 118.

Illustrations from case law include:
  (a) A promise not to use trade secrets or personal influence over customers may be enforced (*Spafax Ltd v Harrison* [1980] I.R.L.R. 442).
  (b) Refusal by the employee to sign such an agreement may be a fair reason for dismissal (*RS Components v Irwin* [1973] I.C.R. 535).
  (c) A promise not to use details of a secret manufacturing process for a period of five years was enforceable (*Forster & Sons Ltd v Suggett* (1918) 35 T.L.R. 87).
  (d) A promise by an engineer not to work for a competitor for a period of seven years was not enforceable. It was held to be an unreasonable restriction on his knowledge and skill (*Herbert Morris Ltd v Saxelby* [1916] 1 A.C. 688).

(e) A promise by a negotiator in an estate agent's office not to work in that industry within a certain geographical area for a certain period of time was held not to be enforceable since the business was of a non-recurring type, and thus the agreement would not protect the employer's existing business, but merely restrain the employee from obtaining work (*Bowler v Lovegrove* [1921] 1 ch.642).

(f) An agreement preventing an employee from working within an industry or organisation in any capacity will generally be void as being wider than is necessary to protect a proprietary interest (*Littlewoods Organisation Ltd v Harris* [1978] 1 All E.R. 1026; *Commercial Plastics Ltd v Vincent* [1965] 1 QB 623).

However:

(g) An agreement preventing an individual from working anywhere in the world, in a particular industry for a period of 25 years was held to be valid, since the promise had been bought for the equivalent of millions of pounds! (*Nordenfelt v Maxim Nordenfelt Guns Co Ltd* [1894] A.C. 535).

(h) An agreement preventing a solicitor's clerk from working for other solicitors within an area of a seven mile radius for the remainder of his life was held to be valid! (*Fitch v Dewes* [1921] 2 A.C. 158)—it is suggested that except in the most exceptional circumstances such an agreement would today be held to be far too wide to be enforceable.

The court will occasionally adopt a "blue pencil" approach to restraint of trade covenants, striking out such parts as are unenforceable, whilst upholding the remainder (*T Lucas & Co Ltd v Mitchell* [1974] Ch.129). This is not the normal approach however, since the courts follow the contract doctrine of *contra proferentum*—in cases of doubt or ambiguity interpreting the clause against the party seeking to rely upon it.

KEY CASE

FACCENDA CHICKEN LTD V FOWLER [1986] I.C.R. 297

Mr Fowler had worked for Faccenda as sales manager, he left and set up his own business in competition, employing several other Faccenda ex-employees. Between them they had information as to the names and addresses of Faccenda's customers, amounts of their orders and the prices charged.

Faccenda argued that this was confidential information, and Fowler should be restrained from using it.

Held: "It is clear that the obligation not to use or disclose information may cover secret processes...and other information which is of a sufficiently high degree of confidentiality as to amount to a trade secret".

The obligation does not extend, however, to cover all information which is given to or acquired by the employee while in his employment, and in particular may not cover information which is only "confidential"...

Commentary

The judgment is worth reading in full for the distinctions it draws between "trade secrets" and other information, which whilst being "confidential", may not be protected once the employment is concluded.

COUNTRYWIDE ASSURED FINANCIAL SERVICES LTD V (1) SMART (2) POLLARD [2004] EWHC 1214

Mr Pollard worked for an estate agent and his contract of employment contained a number of restrictive covenants. One of these covenants purported to restrict him from working for any other estate agent within a three mile radius for a period of three months after the termination of his employment, and another restricted him from soliciting any of Countrywide's clients for a period of six months following termination. Mr Pollard left Countrywide to work for another estate agent in the area, and his former employer sought to enforce the first covenant against him.

Held: Since the second covenant restricted Mr Pollard from soliciting Countrywide's clients for a period of six months and since there was no evidence that Mr Pollard had taken confidential information with him to his new employers, there was no separate protectable interest covered by the second covenant.

Commentary

The courts will only uphold a specific restrictive covenant if relates to a specific protectable interest, and even then, only in so far as that covenant is reasonable. In this case, the court also made the point that an employer's good will is in itself not an interest capable of protection.

Figure 6 Restrictive Covenants

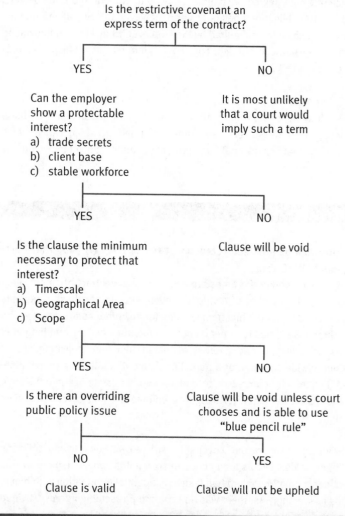

Is the restrictive covenant an express term of the contract?

YES — Can the employer show a protectable interest?
a) trade secrets
b) client base
c) stable workforce

NO — It is most unlikely that a court would imply such a term

YES — Is the clause the minimum necessary to protect that interest?
a) Timescale
b) Geographical Area
c) Scope

NO — Clause will be void

YES — Is there an overriding public policy issue

NO — Clause will be void unless court chooses and is able to use "blue pencil rule"

NO — Clause is valid

YES — Clause will not be upheld

Chapter Checklist

You should now know and understand:

- what is meant by garden leave;

- the relationship between the employee's duty of fidelity and a restrictive covenant;

- the approach of the courts in determining the validity of a restrictive covenant.

The Question

Peter works as a ladies hairdresser in Central Nottingham. His contract of employment contains the following clause: "If for any reason the employee leaves the employer's employment, he (the employee) undertakes not to work in the hairdressing industry within the Nottingham area for a period of one year".

Discuss the enforceability of this clause.

Suggested points for consideration

The court will hold the clause void, unless the employer has a protectable interest and the clause is the minimum necessary to protect that interest. The court will also consider whether the clause offends against public policy.

Protectable interest—the company's client base is an interest capable of protection.

Reasonableness of clause.

(a) scope: the scope appears far too wide; it appears to stop Peter working in any capacity within the entire hairdressing industry.

(b) geographical area: this also appears wide, but perhaps more importantly "Nottingham area" is ambiguous.

(c) timescale: one year is probably longer than necessary to protect the company's interest, a time of (say) three months would perhaps be more appropriate.

There do not appear to be any over-riding public policy issues.
The clause is almost certainly unenforceable as it stands, and the court would not be able to "blue-pencil" the offending parts, nor would they be likely to re-write the clause.

Trade Unions

LEGISLATION HIGHLIGHTER

TRADE UNION AND LABOUR RELATIONS (CONSOLIDATION) ACT 1992
EUROPEAN CONVENTION ON HUMAN RIGHTS ARTICLE 11

A broad definition of a "trade union" is included in s.1 of the Trade Union and Labour Relations (Consolidation) Act 1992 (TULR(C)A). It is an organisation of workers, or an association of such organisations, whose principal purposes include the regulation of relations between those workers and their employers. The courts have defined this definition strictly in such cases as *Midland Cold Storage v Turner* [1972] I.C.R. 773.

Section 10 of the TULR(C)A defines the status of a trade union as "quasi- corporate". As such, it is not a company, a provident society or a friendly society. It is, however, capable of:

(a) making contracts in its own name;

(b) suing and being sued in its own name;

(c) having proceedings brought against it for offences committed by it or on its behalf.

Interestingly, and perhaps strangely, it would appear that a trade union may not however be able to bring an action for defamation in its own name (*EEPTU v Times Newspapers* [1980] 1 All E.R. 1097), although this issue is not totally clear.

Independent Trade Union Status

It is necessary for a trade union to be granted independent status in order for it to gain various statutory rights: automatic employer recognition in certain circumstances, protection of its members against dismissal for union activities, time off for its members to undertake particular union activities, access to information for collective bargaining purposes, etc. An independent trade union is one which is not under the control of, or liable to interference from, an employer. The EAT in the case of *Blue Circle Staff Association v Certification Officer* [1977] 1 W.L.R. 239 laid down a list of guidelines for the Certification Officer when determining the status of a trade union; included in the list are such issues as whether the union is financially independent from the employer, whether the union rule book allows the employer to interfere with, or even control, the union, and whether the union has a "robust attitude in negotiation" with the employer. It is possible for a single-company union to obtain independent status, but both the courts and the Certification Officer are likely to appreciate that such unions are more susceptible to influence from the employer than those unions operating over a range of employers.

Trade Union Recognition

Recognition of a trade union by the relevant employer is important. It entitles the union to involvement in collective bargaining activities, it may claim disclosure of information for such purposes, its representatives and members are entitled to time off for certain union activities, and the union must be consulted on training issues and opportunities. An employer may choose to recognise a union voluntarily, or under the ERelA 1999 there is automatic recognition by an employer of an independent trade union normally if either a majority of the workers in the bargaining unit are members of the trade union, or 40 per cent of those workers in the bargaining unit vote in favour of recognition. The particular rules governing all aspects of statutory recognition are complex. The process for recognition is supervised by the Central Arbitration Committee.

Trade Union Political Funds

If a trade union wishes to contribute towards political ends, such as contributions to political parties, that contribution must come from a separate political fund. This stems from the early days of the Labour Party, at which time Members of Parliament were unpaid, but Labour MPs received money from trade unions. The case of *ASRS v Osborne* [1910] A.C. 87 held that a levy on union members for political purposes was unlawful, but the **Trade Union Act of 1913** subsequently allowed a union to set up a separate political fund into which union members could contribute if they wished. This is still the position today, although legislation has imposed restrictions on unions in terms of periodic ballots for maintaining such funds.

KEY CASE

BIRCH V NATIONAL UNION OF RAILWAYMEN [1950] CH.602
The NUR rulebook contained a rule that only those members contributing to the political fund may take part in the management of that fund. Mr Birch, who chose not to contribute to the political fund, was elected as a local branch official, part of whose duties was an

involvement in the management of the political fund. The union argued that he was not eligible for office, since he would be unable to fulfil all the required duties.

Held: The court held that the rule concerning the political fund offended against, what is now, s.82(1) of the TULR(C)A. Whereas it was reasonable that only those members who contributed to the political fund should have authority to manage the fund, it was quite another thing that the rule should have the effect of disqualifying anyone not contributing to the fund from holding office of almost any sort within the union.

Commentary
The case is one of many examples demonstrating the involvement of the courts in the internal running of trade unions.

Freedom of Association
The right to freedom of association is contained in Art.11 of the ECHR. It includes the "right to freedom of association with others, including the right to form and join trade unions..." However, prior to 1988, in the UK a "closed shop" principle was lawful—in order for a worker to get a job they must be a member of the trade union, should they leave the trade union they may not keep the job. This closed shop principle was outlawed by the Conservative government under Margaret Thatcher in a series of legislative measures during the 1980s. It should be noted that there are some statutory restrictions concerning the ability of certain groups to either join a trade union or to take part in industrial action; police officers are not permitted to join a trade union, although they are automatically members of the Police Federation; members of the armed forces are not permitted to take part in industrial action; and certain Crown employees have a clause in their contracts of employment by which they agree not to join a trade union.

Following the introduction of the Employment Relations Act 2004, it is unlawful for an employer to offer an inducement to a worker to either join or leave a trade union (see *Wilson & Ors v UK* [2002] I.R.L.R. 568).

Young, James and Webster v United Kingdom [1981] I.R.L.R. 408
ECHR
At the time, British Rail operated a closed shop. Employment within British Rail at many levels was only permitted if the employee joined the appropriate trade union; should he refuse to join or subsequently leave the union, his employment would terminate. The three complainants had all refused to join the trade union and had been dismissed by British Rail. They took their case to the ECHR.

Held: The court held that the right to form or join a trade union is a fundamental aspect of freedom of association. Conversely, therefore, the right not to join or to leave a union must also form part of the basic right of freedom of association. The actions of British Rail supported by domestic legislation in the UK therefore breached art.11 of the Convention.

Commentary
It must be remembered that the closed shop principle is no longer lawful in the UK, and also that this case was heard long before the judgments of the ECHR had effect in UK courts or legislation.

Union Rules
The union rules will form part of the contract between the union and its members, as such, both the union rules and disciplinary procedures are open to scrutiny by the courts (*Lee v The Showmen's Guild of Great Britain* [1952] 2 QB 329), and are subject to issues of natural justice (*Roebuck v National Union of Mineworkers (Yorkshire Area)* no.2 [1978] I.C.R. 676).

All individual union members have the right not to be unjustifiably disciplined by the trade union (TULR(C)A s.64). Any union member complaining of unjustified action by the union may present a complaint within three months to an Employment Tribunal.

There have previously been only limited reasons for which a trade union may either exclude a worker from membership of the union, or expel an existing union member. However, in the case of *ASLEF v United Kingdom* [2007] I.R.L.R. 361 (ECtHR) the court held that art.11 of the European Convention on Human Rights should not be interpreted as imposing an obligation on trade unions to allow membership to anyone who wished to join, since refusal to allow membership would not affect an individual's freedom of expression or political activities, nor would it amount to a particular detriment.

Chapter Checklist

You should now know and understand:

- the status of a trade union;
- what is meant by an independent trade union;
- the interpretation by the courts of the scope of Article 11 ECHR;
- the application of union rules.

QUESTION AND ANSWER

The Question

"Legislation, particularly that introduced since the coming to power of the Thatcher government, has severely restricted the actions and powers of self-determination of the trade unions in this country."

Discuss.

Suggested points for consideration

The ambiguous status of trade unions.

The power of the courts to intervene in trade union management.

Legislation restricting how lawful industrial action may be undertaken (perhaps also an overview of the manner in which the Thatcher government restricted the actions of the unions, along with comments concerning legislation enacted by the following Labour governments).

The unions' liability in tort and the widening of the scope of non-protected torts.

Consideration of the effect of Human Rights legislation at national level, followed by the impact of judgments of the EctHR in such cases as *Wilson v Palmer*, and *ASLEF v UK*.

Industrial Action

TRADE UNION AND LABOUR RELATIONS (CONSOLIDATION) ACT 1992
SECTION 219

At common law, all industrial action will amount to a breach of the contract of employment. A strike—withdrawal of labour—will obviously constitute a breach of contract (*Simmons v Hoover Ltd* [1977] I.C.R. 61, as will a work to rule (*Secretary of State for Employment v ASLEF* [1972] 2 All E.R. 949, or indeed a refusal to work non-contractual overtime (*Faust v Power Packing Casemakers Ltd* [1983] I.R.L.R. 117). However, statute has intervened to offer an amount of protection to trade unions and their members in certain situations.

It should be understood that there is no "right to strike" in UK law, but be aware of dicta in cases such as *Wilson v UK*; *Palmer v UK* [2002] I.R.L.R. 568, *UNISON v UK* [2002] I.R.L.R. 497, and more recently the ECHR in *Enerji Yapi-Yol Sen v Turkey* [2009] ECHR 2251 cf *Metrobus Ltd v UNITE* [2009] IRLR 851.

Official and Unofficial Action

It is important to distinguish between official and unofficial industrial action. Official action is that which is supported by the trade union; unofficial action is that which the union has not repudiated. For action to be deemed unofficial, it is not sufficient that the union merely does not support it; the union must actively repudiate the action (*Express and Star Ltd v NGA* [1985] I.R.L.R. 455) by giving immediate notice of repudiation to those organising the action (s.21(2)(a) of the TULR(C)A 1992) and to all union members and their employers who may become involved in the action (s.21(2)(b) of the TULR(C)A 1992,).

One reason for differentiating between official and unofficial action is that if workers are dismissed for taking part in unofficial action the employment tribunal will have no jurisdiction to hear their complaint of unfair dismissal.

The position regarding unfair dismissal for taking part in industrial action is governed by the ss.237–239 of the TULR(C)A 1992.

Dismissal for participation in unofficial action is effectively automatically fair (s.237).

Dismissal for participation in lawful official action is automatically unfair. This protection lasts for eight weeks from the start of the official action (or longer if the employer has failed to take reasonable procedural steps to resolve the dispute, s.238A(6)), after which time the dismissal will be fair, subject to s.238A.

Dismissal for participation in official action which is unlawful, or has lasted over eight weeks at the time of dismissal, is automatically fair, unless:

(i) not all current participants in the action have been dismissed; or

(ii) within three months of the dismissals, some or any (but not all) of those dismissed are selectively re-employed. In such cases the employment tribunal would consider the issue of fairness of dismissal by applying the "reasonableness" test.

Trade Unions' Liability in Tort

The structure of the law in this area is very complex. Perhaps the simplest way of tackling a problem question in this issue it is to adopt a three-stage approach:

(a) Has a tort been committed?

(b) If so, is the action protected by the immunity granted by s.219 of the TULR(C)A 1992?

(c) If so, has the immunity been lost by the union's failure to comply with legislation (mainly ss.222–226 of the TULR(C)A 1992)?

Has a Tort been Committed?

It is important to identify which torts may have been committed during industrial action. The commission of some torts—the major economic torts—may in some circumstances be granted immunity by statute, but the organisers of industrial action, usually the trade union, will still have liability for torts such as public nuisance (*News Group Newspapers Ltd v SOGAT '82* [1986] I.R.L.R. 337).

The Major Economic Torts

The scope of these economic torts has been increased over the years by the courts; the major torts are: inducement of breach of contract; interference with contract; interference with trade or business; intimidation; and conspiracy.

Inducement to Breach of Contract

This tort can take two forms, direct or indirect.

The direct form occurs when an inducement is made by one party, usually the trade union, to the second party, the employee, to breach a contract which the second party has with the third party, the employer. Generally the contract is the employee's contract of employment, and the breach may be a withdrawal of labour—a strike—(*Simmons v Hoover Ltd* [1977] I.C.R. 61), a "go-slow" or work to rule (*British Telecommunications Plc v Ticehurst* [1992] I.C.R. 383) or other form of industrial action (*Wiluszynski v Tower Hamlets LBC* [1989] I.C.R. 493). The generally quoted example of a direct inducement to breach of contract is the old case of *Lumley v Gye* [1853] 2 E. & B. 216, in which an opera singer who was under contract to appear at a particular theatre was persuaded by an agent to break her contract and appear instead at a different theatre. The agent was liable for, what was then, the new tort of inducement to breach of contract.

The indirect form of the tort is slightly more complicated. It requires that party A should induce party B to cause a breach of a contract between parties C and D. An example is the case of *DC Thomson & Co Ltd v Deakin* [1952] ch.646, in which the trade union called upon workers in several companies to refuse to handle deliveries to a particular company, DC Thomson, who were in dispute with the union. Workers from another company, Bowaters, made it clear to their employer that they would not handle deliveries to Thomson's.

Thomson's then sought action against the trade union for the tort of inducement to breach of contract. The court held that the tort would be committed if the following four elements were proved: if the trade union knew of the existence of the contract and intended its breach; if the union did induce a breach of the contract; if the employees so persuaded did indeed breach their contracts of employment; and if the breach of their contracts of employment did cause the breach of the contract complained of. The later case of *Emerald Construction Ltd v Lowthian* [1966] 1 W.L.R. 691 makes it clear that it is not necessary that the union should have any detailed knowledge of the contract, merely that it is aware, or should be aware, in general terms of the existence of such a contract.

It is said that for the indirect form of the tort of inducement to breach of contract "unlawful means" must be used. These unlawful means need be nothing more than another tort themselves. In the case of *DC Thomson* the unlawful means would be the inducement to the workers to breach their contracts of employment—itself the simple or direct form of the tort. To prove the direct form of this tort no unlawful means are necessary. It should be noted that if the "unlawful means" are themselves protected by the immunities under s.219 of the TULR(C)A 1992, they will not constitute unlawful means for the purpose of this tort (see the section on "immunities").

Interference with Contract

This is essentially an extended version of the tort of inducement to breach of contract. The important difference is that it is not necessary to prove an actual breach of a contract. According to Lord Denning in the case of *Torquay Hotel Co Ltd v Cousins* [1969] 2 ch.106, if a person deliberately interferes with the trade or business of another by any means which are unlawful, then a tort will be committed, even though no actual breach of contract may arise.

Interference with Trade or Business

This may be viewed as either a further extension of the torts of inducement to breach of contract and interference with contract, or an "umbrella" tort of which the two previous torts are merely sub-species. Its existence was confirmed by the House of Lords in *Merkur Island Shipping Corp v Laughton* [1983] 2 All E.R. 189, where it was stated that there was no need to prove interference with any particular or specific contract, thus confirming Lord Denning's dicta in *Torquay Hotel* (above). It would therefore be possible to commit this tort by frightening off potential, rather than actual, customers. As with the tort of interference with contract, however, it must be shown that unlawful means have been employed, which in practice will usually simply mean that the commission of this tort has involved the commission of another tort.

Intimidation

Although the courts have long held that the threat of physical violence may constitute an unlawful act, usually a criminal act, it was not until the case of *Rookes v Barnard* [1964] A.C. 1129 that the tort of intimidation was identified through the use of threats of breach of contract. Lord Devlin stated in that case: "I find nothing to differentiate a threat of a breach of contract from a threat of physical violence or other illegal threat." Thus putting pressure on an employer to act in a certain way by threatening to breach a contract, often the contract of employment, will amount to the commission of the tort of intimidation.

Conspiracy

If two or more combine to injure another, and their predominant purpose is to injure the other rather than to advance their own legitimate interests, the tort of conspiracy will be committed. This form of the tort has little practical importance following the case of *Crofter Hand Woven Harris Tweed Co v*

Veitch [1942] A.C. 435, where it was accepted by the House of Lords that normal trade union purposes were "legitimate interests" as long as they were the predominant motive of the organisers of the industrial action. However, if "unlawful means" are used, the defence of legitimate interests will not succeed; it is not clear whether a simple breach of contract would be sufficient to constitute unlawful means for the commission of this tort.

Is the Action Protected by an Immunity?

The Statutory Immunities

Section 219 of the TULR(C)A 1992 provides, to at least some extent, immunity from liability in the commission of all of the above torts. This immunity will only apply where the actions complained of are carried out "in contemplation and furtherance of a trade dispute"—the so-called "Golden Formula".

Section 219(1) states:

An act done by a person in contemplation or furtherance of a trade dispute is not actionable in tort on the ground only—

(a) that it induces another person to break a contract or interferes or induces another person to interfere with its performance, or [thus protecting directly against Inducement of Breach of Contract and Interference with Contract and indirectly against Interference with Business by limiting the scope for "unlawful means"]

(b) that it consists in his threatening that a contract (whether one to which he is a party or not) will be broken or its performance interfered with, or that he will induce another person to break a contract or interfere with its performance. [thus protecting directly against Intimidation and indirectly against Inducement of Breach of Contract, Interference with Contract and Interference with Business by limiting the scope for "unlawful means"]

Section 219(2) states:

An agreement or combination by two or more persons to do or procure the doing of an act in contemplation or furtherance of a trade dispute is not actionable in tort if the act is one which if done without any such agreement or combination would not be actionable in tort. [thus protecting directly against conspiracy to injure without the use of unlawful means and also conspiracy to use unlawful means except where it is an agreement to commit a tort].

The Golden Formula

Protection under s.219 is only granted to those actions which are carried out in contemplation or furtherance of a trade dispute.

A trade dispute is defined in s.244 of the TULR(C)A 1992 as a dispute between workers and their employer which relates wholly or mainly to such issues as terms and conditions of employment.

It would thus exclude disputes where the union is motivated mainly by "political" considerations, e.g. ideological objections to privatisation (*Mercury Communications Ltd v Scott-Garner* [1984] I.C.R. 741), or refusing to handle mail for South Africa as an anti-apartheid protest (*Gouriet v UPOW* [1978] A.C. 435), as well as disputes motivated mainly by personal spite (*Torquay Hotels Ltd v Cousins* [1969] 2 ch.106; *Huntley v Thornton* [1957] 1 All E.R. 234).

"In Contemplation" requires the dispute to be imminent—*Bent's Brewery Co Ltd v Hogan* [1945] 2 All E.R. 570.

"In Furtherance" presupposes a dispute already in existence and not yet over (see, e.g. *Stewart v AUEW* [1973] I.C.R. 128). An action is in furtherance of the dispute if D genuinely believes it will further its interests in the dispute whether or not it will or is capable of doing so and whether or not it is a reasonable means of doing so (*Express Newspapers Ltd v McShane* [1980] I.C.R. 42; *NWL Ltd v Woods* [1979] 1 W.L.R. 1294).

Has the Immunity been Lost?

The statutory immunities contained in s.219 will be lost if any of the requirements contained in the legislation, mainly in ss.222–234 TULR(C)A 1992, are breached. This covers such issues as:

(a) taking action to enforce union membership (s.222);
(b) taking action due to the dismissal of an employee for taking unofficial industrial action (s.223);
(c) if the action amounts to secondary action (s.224);
(d) if the action is to impose union recognition (s.225); or
(e) if the extensive requirements concerning the organisation of the ballot have not been met (ss.226–234)—the rules covering balloting are complex, but have been somewhat clarified by the ERelA 1999 and the ERelA 2004.

If the immunities have been lost, or if torts have been committed which are not covered by the protection afforded by s.219, the trade union may be liable for damages in a civil action for tort. For a recent example illustrating some of the complexities of these issues see *National Union of Rail, Maritime & Transport Workers v Serco Ltd* [2011] IRLR 399 CA.

Picketing

Section 220 of the TULR(C)A states:

"It is lawful for a person in contemplation or furtherance of a trade dispute to attend—(a) at or near his own place of work, or (b) if he is an official of a trade union, at or near the place of work of a member of the union whom he is accompanying and whom he represents, for the purpose only of peacefully obtaining or communicating information, or peacefully persuading any person to work or abstain from working."

It should therefore be noted that:

(a) the picketing must come within the Golden Formula,

(b) the picketing must be at or near the pickets' workplace—in the case of *Rayware Ltd v TGWU* [1989] I.R.L.R. 134, the Court of Appeal held that this should be the closest point to their workplace at which the pickets could lawfully assemble,

(c) picketing is for clearly defined purposes only—in the case of *Broome v DPP* [1974] I.C.R. 84 a picket was arrested for attempting to stop a vehicle entering his employer's premises.

(d) picketing must be peaceful—a large number of pickets could not be said to be "peacefully communicating", their purpose was to intimidate (*Thomas v NUM* [1985] I.R.L.R. 136), in which the court restricted picket numbers to a maximum of six.

Certainly there is relevance within Arts 10 and 11 ECHR to the issue of picketing, but as yet these have not been fully tested in law.

Employer's Remedies against Individual Employee Participants

Apart from any remedy the employer may have against the trade union—generally either injunction or action in tort for damages—the employer may also have remedies against the individual employee.

(a) The courts will not grant the remedy of specific performance against an employee (s.236 of the TULR(C)A 1992).

(b) Damages may be awarded, but only for the individual's own contribution to the loss, so such a remedy is not usually sought in practice (*NCB v Galley* [1958] 1 W.L.R. 16).

(c) Deductions from wages, amounting in effect to self-assessed damages and permitted under s.14(5) of the ERA 1996, see for example *Miles v Wakefield* MDC [1987] I.C.R. 368 and *Wiluszynski v London Borough of Tower Hamlets* [1989] I.C.R. 493.

(d) Dismissal at common law may be contractually permitted without notice where, as will usually be the case, employee's action is a repudiatory breach. However, whether or not the action is in breach of contract, the position concerning unfair dismissal is governed by ss.237-9 of the TULR(C)A 1992 which distinguish between official (i.e. backed by his TU) and unofficial action (see above).

Chapter Checklist

You should now know and understand:

- the meaning of industrial action;
- the difference between official and unofficial action;
- the scope of liability for trade unions undertaking industrial action;
- what is meant by "the golden formula";
- the ways in which a union may lose its immunity for liability;
- the law relating to picketing.

QUESTION AND ANSWER

The Question

A union institutes strike action for its members employed by XCo, following the breakdown of talks between XCo and the union concerning pay increases. XCo is unable to fulfill its contract to supply one of its clients, YCo. YCo seeks damages from the union in respect of its loss of business caused by XCo's inability to supply.

Discuss the legal position.

Suggested points for consideration

Is the union an independent trade union?

Has a tort been committed? ("interference with trade or business"—*Merkur Island Shipping*).

Is the union's action protected by the "golden formula" (s.219 TULR(C)A 1992)?

Has that protection been lost (is the action "official industrial action", have all of the correct procedures been carried out under ss.222–226 TULR(C)A 1992)?

Handy Hints and Useful Websites

17

Examination questions in employment law usually take one of two forms; either essay questions or problem questions. These are very different, both in format and in what is required of the examinee, and we will look at each type of question in turn.

Students usually prefer one type of question to the other, the majority normally opting for the problem question. Unfortunately for many students, examinations are usually set in a way that requires the student to attempt at least one of each style of question.

Very few, if any, questions ever require the student to write all he or she knows about a topic, and it is very possible for even the most knowledgeable student to make a poor showing in an examination by simply not answering the question that has been asked. Fortunately, answering examination questions is a skill, and like any other skill, it may be learned.

Before going into the examination room you will probably know both how long the examination lasts and how many questions you are required to answer; if so, work out in advance how much time you can afford to spend on each question—and stick to it! The first 20 per cent or 30 per cent of marks are the easiest to get and are normally obtainable in the first few minutes of your answer, after that, marks become progressively more difficult to obtain; so don't be tempted to spend half of your time on the first of three questions and find yourself with no time for the third! Don't forget to allow for several minutes reading time, ideally both at the start and at the end of the examination.

Many examinations allow you to take an unannotated statute book into the examination room. Make full use of this by ensuring that you are familiar with the layout and format of the book beforehand—specific statute referencing may gain you several marks, and in some questions, e.g. redundancy, statute should be your starting point.

Once inside the examination room the most basic rule to remember when presented with an examination paper is that putting pen to paper is one of the last things you should do!

The following format may help:

(a) Read through the paper. Pay particular attention to the instructions.

(b) Read through the paper again, deciding which questions to answer, and perhaps making brief preliminary notes.

(c) Prepare an answer plan. Read through the answer plan ensuring that it answers the question asked.

(d) Write your answer, supporting each proposition with an authority of either statute or case law.

(e) Read through your answer, making sure that what you are reading is what you have written, and that what you have written is what you meant to write.

(f) If you have time remaining, re-read both the question and answer—just to be on the safe side!

(g) Finally, an obvious point, if you do start to run out of time, answer in note form—don't simply give up, it is surprising how many relevant points you can make in just five minutes writing time.

ESSAY QUESTIONS

Although most students seem to prefer problem questions to essay questions, a well answered essay question is probably more likely to gain better marks than a well answered problem. The advantage to an essay question, assuming you have a good knowledge of your subject, is that you are not as constrained by the question and you have more opportunity to develop ideas and approaches. However, the same rules apply to both types of question: support your arguments with authorities, and ensure that you understand what the question requires of you.

If you are not confident in the topic, or if you are not sure what is required by the examiner, you would be well advised not to attempt that essay question.

Style of writing, and, to some extent, the structure of your answer are personal matters. Trying to imitate another's style is unlikely to be successful, and whilst it is all very well to say that an essay should have a start, a middle and an end, not all essay questions lend themselves to that treatment.

What is important—apart from content, which is essential—is ensuring that you write legibly, with decent grammar and reasonable spelling, so that the examiner can not only read what you have written, but can also understand what you mean.

As with all examination questions, it is very important that you re-read what you have written. Don't make the mistake once you have finished the exam of staring out of the window or leaving early—use any time remaining to re-read and re-check.

PROBLEM QUESTIONS

The advantage to a problem question is that you are given much more information in the question on which to base your answer. Assuming you understand what the question requires of you, and you have knowledge of the topic, the main problem is how to structure your answer. The two important factors are:

(a) a good answer plan, and

(b) plenty of practice.

USEFUL WEBSITES

British and Irish Legal Information Institute
www.bailii.org

Court of Justice of the European Communities
http://curia.europa.eu

Daily Law Notes
www.iclr.co.uk

Employment Appeals Tribunal
www.employmentappeals.gov.uk

European Court of Human Rights
www.echr.coe.int/echr

Her Majesty's Courts Service
www.hmcourts-service.gov.uk

The Times
www.timesonline.co.uk

Index